"The Star Spangled Banner"

Da Capo Press Music Reprint Series

GENERAL EDITOR

FREDERICK FREEDMAN

VASSAR COLLEGE

"The Star Spangled Banner"

BY

OSCAR GEORGE THEODORE SONNECK

𝄞 DA CAPO PRESS · NEW YORK · 1969

A Da Capo Press Reprint Edition

This Da Capo Press edition of
"The Star Spangled Banner"
is an unabridged republication of the first edition
published in Washington, D. C., in 1914.

Library of Congress Catalog Card Number 68-16245

Published by Da Capo Press
A Division of Plenum Publishing Corporation
227 West 17th Street
New York, N.Y. 10011

Printed in the United States of America

"The Star Spangled Banner"

FRANCIS SCOTT KEY.

1780–1843.

(By courtesy of the Maryland Historical Society.)

LIBRARY OF CONGRESS

"The Star Spangled Banner"

(Revised and enlarged from the "Report" on the above
and other airs, issued in 1909)

BY

OSCAR GEORGE THEODORE SONNECK

CHIEF OF THE DIVISION OF MUSIC

WASHINGTON
GOVERNMENT PRINTING OFFICE
1914

L. C. card, 13–35008

PREFATORY NOTE

In December, 1907, I received instructions from the Librarian of Congress to "bring together the various versions both of text and of music with notes as to the historical evolution" of "The Star Spangled Banner," "Hail Columbia," "America," and "Yankee Doodle." The result was the special "Report" issued by the Library in 1909. In form it was frankly not such a history of the subject as one would write for popular consumption. In it data were collected, eliminated, or verified; popular theories founded on these data were analyzed, their refutation or acceptance was suggested, and, of course, some theories of my own were offered for critical consideration. All this was done in such a form that the reader was at no step supposed to find a locked door between himself and the argument. He was not expected to accept a single statement of fact or argument unless the evidence submitted compelled him to do so. This *plein air* treatment of a popular theme distinguished the "Report" somewhat from the bulk of the literature on the subject, and I concluded the prefatory note by saying: "In short, though not intended for popular consumption, it may be used for popular consumption with reasonable assurance of accuracy."

The words "reasonable assurance of accuracy" were not intended to convey the impression that the author had spoken the last word on every phase of the history of the songs treated in his "Report." Sometimes forced to find a way out of a dark labyrinth of conflicting testimony, he knew better than any reader of his "Report" could possibly know, how complicated certain matters were. Often he could not go beyond his authorities. They were fallible and their errors became his, unless he detected them. Detection was not always so very simple as it may look to those whose ambition it is to clear just one of innumerable points. However, the author hoped that his "Report" would lead to the discovery of new data, that would facilitate the solution of certain problems which he could only treat at the time with critical caution and without committing the reader to his personal impressions. This hope has been fulfilled. The "Report" of 1909 undoubtedly stimulated a revival of interest in the history of the songs discussed. With this revival of interest came renewed search for hidden data and a lively controversy arose as to whether or not John Stafford Smith composed "To Anacreon in Heaven."

In view of the probability that in September, 1914, Francis Scott Key's memory would be honored by numerous celebrations of the centenary of his "Star Spangled Banner," the Library of Congress decided to issue the chapter on his national song separately in a revised and enlarged edition.   It was to embody the principal literature on the subject since 1909.   The principle and method of treatment were to be exactly the same as in the "Report" of 1909.   This accounts for the *technique* adopted and for much that would be unnecessary and unskillful in a plain historical narrative.

If in the discussion now and then a word has fallen with a sting to it, the reader, it is hoped, will appreciate how difficult it sometimes is, even in a governmental "Report" to suppress entirely the personal note.   After all, Government officials are human beings and facts do not always speak for themselves.   To use a musical simile, in a complicated orchestral composition often much depends on the instrumentation of the thematic idea.   Its development may be entirely logical, but, unless it be given to some instrument of piercing tone, it may in that particular moment not reach the ears of the audience at all.

O. G. SONNECK
Chief, Music Division

HERBERT PUTNAM
Librarian of Congress
Washington, D. C., January, 1914

POSTSCRIPT

This book was ready for the binder when word reached me that the discussion between Father Henry and Dr. Grattan Flood would be continued in the June number of the "American Catholic Historical Society of Philadelphia Records."   The conclusions reached in my book are not affected in the slightest thereby, inasmuch as Dr. Grattan Flood admittedly was unable to prove his sudden and startling theory that "To Anacreon in Heaven" was sung at Dublin in 1762 and at Edinburgh in 1755.   From data since searched for me in Dublin sources, but received too late for insertion in this edition of my book, I have gained the impression that Dr. Grattan Flood was misled into his theory by some unfortunate but pardonable error in his notes.

O. G. SONNECK

WIESBADEN, *June, 1914*

CONTENTS

INTRODUCTORY REMARKS.

In the "Report on 'The Star-Spangled Banner,' 'Hail Columbia,' 'America,' 'Yankee Doodle'" (Washington, Government Printing Office, 1909), the chapter on "The Star-Spangled Banner" began with an account of the origin of Francis Scott Key's poem. This was followed by a brief summary of the European and American history of the tune "To Anacreon in Heaven," to which "The Star-Spangled Banner" is sung, by a comparative investigation of extant manuscripts of Key's poem, and finally by a survey of the different versions of the melody as now in use. For this revised and enlarged edition of the chapter a division into two independent sections was found to be more logical and convenient, one on "To Anacreon in Heaven," the other on "The Star-Spangled Banner" proper.

As a prelude to this chapter it is not necessary, but it may not be inadvisable to state, in view of certain tendencies to the contrary in the matter of "The Star-Spangled Banner," that research in musical history, in common with every other kind of historical research, aims solely at the orderly establishment of facts and the logical interpretation of available facts. Such facts or the conclusions from such facts may not always be welcome, but the historian is or should be a seeker after historical truth, often enough stranger and more "romantic" than fiction. He should never allow possible preferences of his compatriots or his personal idiosyncrasies to obscure his historical vision.

For instance, every patriotic American would rejoice, with the author of this "Report," if it could be shown by documentary or other unimpeachable evidence that "The Star-Spangled Banner," both in words and music, was of American origin. If that can not be shown, then every patriotic American will be sensible enough not to betray irritation of his patriotic pride because the music of our "Star-Spangled Banner" had its origin in some "monarchical" country of Europe, whether that be Turkey, Russia, Germany, France,

7

England, or Ireland. Nor is there any patriotic reason, so far as I can see, why the citizens of the republican United States of America, founded by men of English, German, Irish, or other descent, and fought for by Irishmen against Irishmen, Englishmen against Englishmen, Germans against Germans, should be expected to smart under the theory that "To Anacreon in Heaven" was of English, not of Irish, French, or German, origin, and to prefer, for instance, an Irish to an English composer. We took the air and we kept it. Transplanted on American soil, it thrived. As "To Anacreon in Heaven" of European origin the air is obsolete and extinct; as the air of "The Star-Spangled Banner," it stirs the blood of every American, regardless of his origin or the origin of the air.

JOHN STAFFORD SMITH.

Engraved (with permission) by T. Illman, from the Original Drawing,
by W. Behnes, in the possession of Mr. Richd. Clarke.

Published by T. Williams, for the Harmonist in Miniature.

1750–1836.

(By courtesy of the British Museum.)

TO ANACREON IN HEAVEN

For methodological reasons it will be best to first submit, with as little preliminary comment as possible, the different theories on the origin and authorship of the song. If at all of a critical bend of mind, the reader will not fail to notice how these different theories either strengthen or weaken each other in certain details, without being subjected to critical cross-examination. He will further notice how some of these theories not only contradict each other, but how full they are of contradictions within themselves, not to mention the amusing spectacle of one and the same author presenting within three years two totally different theories and both times with equally emphatic assertiveness. The survey of theories will be followed by a survey of the bibliographical history of the song, i. e., extant versions of the song in British eighteenth century publications, so far as known to me, will be examined with an attempt to establish their chronological order.

This method of procedure will permit the automatic elimination of obvious nonsense. It will clear the path for a critical analysis of the controversy on John Stafford Smith's authorship of the air and it will enable the critical reader to accept or reject the conclusions reached by me in a fairly complicated structure of argument.

In Notes and Queries, second series, 1861, volume 12, page 310, there appeared a note on "The Star-Spangled Banner" by one "Uneda" to the effect that—

> This song, which is now to be heard everywhere in the United States, is sung to the tune of "Anacreon in Heaven." Was there not a still older song to this tune, commencing "When Bibo went down to the regions below?" It has been stated that this song was an Irish bacchanalian song.[a] Is the air Irish? Is it known who was the composer of it?

---

[a] In the context "this song" refers to "When Bibo, " not "To Anacreon in Heaven."
Two versions of the text of "When Bibo" appear to exist. In the Vocal Magazine, 1778, on page 7 appears as "Song 6. A two-part song. Written by Mr. Prior. *When Bibo thought fit from the world to retreat*" (one stanza of six lines, no tune indicated). The three-stanza text of "When Bibo went down to the regions below," as comparison will show, is merely an amplified paraphrase of Prior's text. In the Universal Songster, Volume III, London [1827], there appears the "When Bibo went down" text with note "Air: To Anacreon in Heaven." I tried to sing the text to the air, but I failed, except for the first few lines, which go well with "To Anacreon in

I pass on to a note on "The Star Spangled Banner" contributed to Notes and Queries (3d ser., 1864, vol. 6, pp. 429–430) by William Pinkerton. He did not pretend to know the composer of the "old English song" "To Anacreon in Heaven," but he rendered us a service by mentioning several parodies of "To Anacreon," as for instance, "*Britannia*—To Neptune enthroned, as he governed the sea," "*Satan's visit to the Jacobine Club*—To old Satan in Hell, where he sat in full glee" [a] and again, as sung to the same tune, "When Bibo went down," mentioning both versions of the text.

For a long time the tune of "To Anacreon in Heaven" was often attributed, if attributed to any particular composer at all, to Dr. Samuel Arnold (1740–1802). Of this opinion were J. C. (in Baltimore Clipper, 1841), Nason (1869), Salisbury (1872), and others. The general inability to substantiate this rumor finally led to one of the most grotesquely absurd articles in musical literature, namely, that in the American Art Journal, 1896 (vol. 68, whole no. 1729, pp. 194–195), by J. Fairfax McLaughlin, under the title "The Star-Spangled Banner. Who composed the music for it? It is American, not English." Mr. McLaughlin challenged any man to point out an

---

Heaven." Others may find it possible to stretch the "To Anacreon in Heaven" melody so as to cover the long "When Bibo went down" stanza.

In Davidson's Universal Melodist, Volume I, London, 1847, "When Bibo went down" is printed with the note "The words by Thomas Dibdin. The music by Travers." This melody runs

When Bi - bo went down   to the re - gions be - low, when   Le - the

(This downward movement of the melody obviously fits the words better than the upward movement of the "Anacreon in Heaven" melody. This is another reason why I believe that the editor of the Universal Songster was mistaken.)

Davidson attributed this melody to John Travers (1703–June, 1758), but in Travers' "Eighteen canzonets, for two, and three voices: the words chiefly by M. Prior," first published at London about 1745, text and melody of "Canzonet IV. An epigram by Matt. Prior" run as follows:

When   Bi - bo .   thought fit   from the world   to   re - treat

and the same melody appeared in the later separate issues of Travers' "favourite canzonets"!

[a] This parody appears to be identical with the one printed without music, so Mr. Frank Kidson informed me on November 29, 1913, in "The Myrtle and The Vine," 1803, Volume II, page 126, as "Satan's visit to the Jacobine Club."

English publication of "To Anacreon in Heaven" prior to that of "words and music" by Matthew Carey in his Vocal Magazine, Philadelphia, 1796 (a book of mysterious whereabouts, by the way, as will appear later). Mr. McLaughlin further found "after a rather exhaustive search" that the first publication of the song in Great Britain occurred in the Universal Songster, "published at London from 1825 to 1834." From this faulty claim of first appearance in America Mr. McLaughlin reached out for the conclusion: "The air as well as the words of our national anthem appear to belong not to England but to the United States."

In view of such naïve and rather irritating ignorance it was easy for *X.* in the Musical Times, of London, 1896 (pp. 516–519) to challenge Mr. McLaughlin to mortal combat and to elaborately bury his patriotic aspirations. The same service could have been rendered him just as neatly and more quickly by a simple reference to the footnote on page 6 of Mr. Stephen Salisbury's "Essay on the Star-Spangled Banner," 1873, where the contents of a pertinent letter from Mr. William Chappell, the distinguished English music merchant and scholar, were made public or to an occasional article contributed by Mr. Chappell to Notes and Queries, 1873 (fourth ser., vol. 11, pp. 50–51), from which I quote the following:

> In the second half of the last century a very jovial society, called The Anacreontic, held its festive and musical meetings at the Crown and Anchor Tavern in the Strand, "a large and curious house, with good rooms and other convenience, fit for entertainments", says Strype. It is now the Whittington Club, but in the last century it was frequented by such men as Dr. Johnson, Boswell, Sir Joshua Reynolds, and Dr. Percy, especially to sup there. A certain Ralph Tomlinson, Esq., was at one time president of the Anacreontic Society, and he wrote the words of the song adopted by the club, while John Stafford Smith set them to music.
>
> The style of the club will be best exemplified by the first and last stanzas of the song. [Then follow these two stanzas of "To Anacreon in Heaven."] The last two lines of each stanza were repeated in chorus.
>
> One of the early editions of the words and music is entitled "The Anacreontic Song, as sung at the Crown and Anchor Tavern in the Strand, the words by Ralph Tomlinson, Esq., late President of that Society. Price 6d. Printed by Longman & Broderip, No. 26, Cheapside, and No. 13, Haymarket." Here the author of the music is unnamed, but it is in "A fifth Book of Canzonets, Catches, Canons, and Glees, sprightly and plaintive. . . . by John Stafford Smith, Gent., of His Majesty's Chapels Royal, author of the favourite glees, 'Blest pair of Sirens,' 'Hark the hollow Woods,' and of 'The Anacreontic,' and other popular songs. Printed for the author, and sold at his house, No. 7, Warwick Street, Spring Gardens, and at the music shops." At page 33 of this collection is "The Anacreontic Song," harmonized by the author.
>
> I have not referred to Stationers' Hall for the date of the Anacreontic Song, but the words and music are included in *Calliope, or the Musical Miscellany,* published in Edinburgh, in 1788, 8vo.; and, before that, they were published in *The Edinburgh Musical Miscellany,* of which the date is torn off in my copy. If any regard to copyright was paid in those publications (which is by no means

certain), the fourteen years of author's right must then have expired, and the date of the song would be between 1770 and 1775. According to the *Biographical Dictionary of Musicians*, John Stafford Smith was born "about 1750," was the son of the organist of Gloucester Cathedral, and was afterwards a pupil of Dr. Boyce—probably in the Chapel Royal, as ultimately he became a gentleman of the Chapels. With such an education he might well have composed the music between the ages of twenty and twenty-five. The contrary motion between the voice part and the bass shows the musician.

Mr. Chappell had not included "To Anacreon in Heaven" in his standard work, "Old English Popular Music," and so Mr. H. Ellis Woolbridge had no occasion to include the above account in his revised edition (1893) of Chappell's lastingly useful work. Otherwise certain inaccuracies probably would have disappeared from Chappell's account. However, on the whole his short, occasional article has the earmarks of correctness, and his deductions were accepted until recently as logical so far as Smith's authorship of the air is concerned. They were followed, for instance, by Mr. Frank Kidson in Grove's Dictionary of Music and Musicians, 1908. In his necessarily brief article, Mr. Kidson dated Smith's Fifth Book as "circa 1780," called attention to the claims of American origin, and, as had done *X.* in the Musical Times, pointed out the appearance of the text of the poem in The Vocal Magazine, 1778.

In the book on "English Music (1604 to 1904), being the lectures given at the Music Loan Exhibition of the Worshipful Company of Musicians, held at Fishmongers' Hall, London Bridge, June–July, 1904," London, 1906, Mr. William H. Cummings in his lecture on "Our English Songs" had this to say on page 51:

> I would fain dwell on this union of race, this marriage of heart and voice, and will therefore call your attention to a song, the product of an Englishman, which has, by adoption, become one of the national songs of our kith and kin on the other side of the Atlantic. "The Star-Spangled Banner," beloved by all our brethren in the United States, was originally composed by John Stafford Smith, in London, about 1750, for a club which met at the "Crown and Anchor" Tavern in the Strand. The club was called the "Anacreontic", and for its social gatherings the president, Ralph Tomlinson, wrote an ode commencing "To Anacreon in Heaven". This was first published without a composer's name, but shortly afterwards Smith brought out a collection of Canzonets, Catches, and Glees, which he sold at his house, 7 Warwick Street, Spring Gardens. In this volume, which contained *only* compositions by himself, we find "To Anacreon in Heaven." The music of the Anacreon ode and that of "The Star-Spangled Banner" is the same. I have brought a copy of the original publication of the ode . . . [On p. 52 the air with words of first stanza is added in C major. On pp. 65–66 Mr. Cummings says and this with the above is all he says on "To Anacreon in Heaven:"]
>
> The volume which contains the original publication of [M. Arne's] "The lass with the delicate air", and also "To Anacreon in Heaven", I have here. It is a very remarkable collection of 116 sheet-songs, put together in the years 1778–82. Amongst other curios are some songs "printed and sold by H. Fougt, at the 'Lyre and Owl', in St. Martin's Lane, near Long-acre. The choicest ballads at a penny a piece, or eighteen for a shilling." There would have been no room for the street pirates in those days.

This brief account has been inserted here for reasons that will appear later.   Mr. Cummings's date "about 1750" may be merely a misprint, because John Stafford Smith (*1750*–1836) can not very well have composed anything "about 1750," because the "Anacreontic Society" did not exist until about 15 years later, and because the title page of the collection of canzonets, etc., mentioned by Mr. Cummings (Smith's Fifth Book) can not have been published until after Smith had been appointed a "Gent. of His Majesty's Chapels Royal" on December 16, 1784.   The significance of this last fact, though plainly put forth in both editions of Grove's Dictionary, escaped me at the time of writing my "Report" in 1909, as it had escaped Mr. Chappell in 1873.   The entry in Grove was called to my attention by Mr. W. H. Grattan Flood in a letter of date December 29, 1909.

End of May, 1909, Mr. A. H. RoSewig, of Philadelphia, copyrighted a 4-page folio sheet with title "Anacreon in Heaven.   The origin of 'The Star Spangled-Banner' with its complete history, by A. H. RoSewig, Mus. Doc."   In this article, which originally had appeared in the Philadelphia North American, Sunday, February 14, 1909, Mr. RoSewig lays claim to sundry discoveries in support of John Stafford Smith's authorship of the "To Anacreon in Heaven" air. As a matter of fact, Mr. RoSewig discovered nothing that was not known to others and accessible in the printed literature on the subject.   The center of interest in his article is held by a twentieth century transcript of "The Anacreontic Song" with title and imprint in type, as if in imitation of that used by Anne Lee, Dublin, in her publication of the song.   However, Mr. RoSewig has added the date "Anno 1780" to the imprint, which contains no such date in Anne Lee's publication, and his transcript of the song is followed (in type, not in manuscript) by the remark "Also harmonised by the author in his Fifth Book of Popular Songs, Catches, etc., page 33."   I feel confident that if Mr. RoSewig had foreseen how these additions to his transcript of "To Anacreon in Heaven" might create confusion, as they did, that he would have preferred to print a photographic facsimile of Anne Lee's publication instead of a transcript with misleading comment.

To this article of Mr. RoSewig's the editor of Church Music (a very excellent magazine, now unfortunately defunct) drew attention in the miscellaneous "Notes" of the May number, 1909.   Thereupon he received from Mr. W. H. Grattan Flood, of Ennisworthy, Ireland, an article called "The original air of The Star-Spangled Banner" with subheading "Notes on the Origin of To Anacreon in Heaven," and this article appeared in Church Music, September, 1909, pages 281–282.   Except for the introductory remarks, it is identical with manuscript "Notes on the origin of To Anacreon in Heaven" sent me under date of June 5, 1908, by Mr. Grattan Flood during the course of a correspondence with him and other British authors on certain phases of the "Star-Spangled Banner" subject. These "Notes" came to me so unsolicited and unexpected that I thanked Mr. Grattan Flood under date of June 29, 1909, for "having gone out of his way to help me." In my "Report" of 1909, "while fully appreciating the courtesy of Mr. W. H. Grattan Flood in transmitting these notes," I regretted "the inadvisability of using them, except in connection with other sources, because these notes are singularly at variance with the contents of several letters sent me by Mr. Grattan Flood on the same subject, and because these notes contain certain positive statements without reference to source which it would be unmethodical to accept unreservedly."

Mr. Grattan Flood's article in Church Music reads as follows:

THE ORIGINAL AIR OF "THE STAR-SPANGLED BANNER."

In the May issue of Church Music I find a correspondent belauding the recent discovery of the original composer of the air to which the "Star-Spangled Banner" is sung. This announcement is somewhat belated. It is now some six years since I examined the Dublin printed copy of the original song "To Anacreon in Heaven," and I also examined the copy containing the information that the music was composed by John Stafford Smith. In June, 1904—over five years ago—Dr. Cummings, in his lecture on "Old English Songs" at the Music Loan Exhibition in London, proved conclusively that Smith was the composer, and exhibited a copy of the setting which Smith, in 1771, sold at his house, No. 7 Warwick Street, Spring Gardens. This lecture is included in *English Music*, published by Charles Scribner's Sons, New York, in the admirable "Music Story Series."

In January, 1908, I was asked by Mr. O. G. Sonneck, head of the Music Division in the Library of Congress at Washington, D. C., to write some notes on "Yankee Doodle" (proving it an Irish air) and on the original air to which the Anacreontic ode was sung, to form part of an official report on the National Airs of America to be presented to Congress.[a] I herewith subjoin my notes on "To Anacreon in Heaven," as, doubtless, they will prove of interest to many readers of Church Music. It is worthy of note that while "Yankee Doodle" is of Irish origin the "Star-Spangled Banner" had its provenance in England.

NOTES ON THE ORIGIN OF "TO ANACREON IN HEAVEN."

There is much confusion as to the authorship of the song "To Anacreon in Heaven." However, it is now tolerably certain that the song was written by Ralph Tomlinson in 1770 or 1771, as the charter song of the Anacreontic Society.

As to the melody, it was composed by John Stafford Smith, a pupil of Dr. Boyce, in 1771.

There is no doubt as to the fact that Ralph Tomlinson wrote the song in the winter of 1770. He was president of the Anacreontic Society, which met in the

---

[a] But compare my statement above. Furthermore, far from accepting Mr. Grattan Flood's theory of the identity of the Irish tune "All the Way to Galway" with "Yankee Doodle," a comparison of the two tunes (see my "Report" of 1909, pp. 146–150) has demonstrated, I believe, to the satisfaction of most everybody except Mr. Grattan Flood, that the two tunes are characteristically different. This difference does not, of course, preclude the possibility of an Irish origin of "Yankee Doodle."

Crown and Anchor Tavern, London, and there is ample evidence that his song was sung from 1771 onwards. The words were printed on broadsides, and appeared in the *Vocal Magazine* for 1778. Four years later (1782) Mr. Mulis was appointed President, and he sang the charter song on several occasions in the years 1782–3. At a later meeting on January 10th, 1791, Haydn was present when the song was sung. The Anacreontic Society was dissolved in 1796.

Elson in his *National Music of America*, and again in his *History of American Music*, says that the composer of the tune to which "To Anacreon" was sung, was either Dr. Arnold or John Stafford Smith, and he waxes merry at the thought that "there is no tune resembling it in Smith's *Musica Antiqua*"—quite oblivious of the fact that Smith's work of that name contained only music "from the 12th to the beginning of the 18th century."

Smith was in his 21st year when he composed the music in 1770–1, and internal evidence clearly points to the influence of Boyce, under whom he was then studying, and some of the phrases are strongly reminiscent of Boyce's "Heart of Oak."

The words and music of "To Anacreon" were published by Longman and Broderip in 1779–1780, and were reprinted by Anne Lee of Dublin (?1780) in 1781. Dr. Cummings says that he saw a copy printed by Henry Fought—at least it is made up with single sheet songs printed by Fought—but this is scarcely likely, as Fought did not print after 1770, and the song and music were not in existence till 1770–71. The copy in the *Vocal Magazine* (1778) has no music.

The most decisive proof of the fact that the tune was composed by Smith is that he includes it in his *Fifth Collection of Canzonets, Catches, etc.*, in 1781. (His name does not appear in Longman and Broderip's issue, nor in that of Anne Lee in 1780). The song with music was published by Brown, of Perth (Scotland), in his *Musical Miscellany*, in 1786. A copy of this rare book is in the writer's musical library. Two years later it appeared in *Calliope* (1788).

Apparently the song (and tune) was brought to America about the year 1790, and it was sung on August 10, 1796, at Savannah, as chronicled by Mr. O. J. Sonneck in his admirable *Early Concert Life in America*. No doubt, it was sung in 1795 and subsequently by the Columbian Anacreontic Society. Anyhow, it was popularized in America between the years 1795 and 1797, and at length was adapted by Paine in May, 1798, for "Adams and Liberty," printed in 1798.

Holden of Dublin printed the Anacreontic Song to Masonic words in 1796, and it was reprinted in 1802. Elson's copy of what he styles the "Original Music" is not quite correct.

(Signed)   W. H. Grattan Flood,
Mus. D., K. S. G., M. R. I. A.

Enniscorthy, *June 5th, 1908.*

A tone of finality sounds through this article, but the same tone of finality is even louder in an article, *again by Mr. W. H. Grattan Flood*, which appeared in the magazine Ave Maria on July 6, 1912, pages 19–20, under the title of "The Irish origin of the tune of The Star-Spangled Banner." In this article, drawn to my attention by Rev. H. T. Henry, of Philadelphia, formerly editor of Church Music, Mr. W. H. Grattan Flood says:

It being, therefore, admitted as beyond any question that Francis Scott Key adapted his song to the tune of "Anacreon in Heaven," the question remains as to the origin of the tune. Mr. Sonneck is wrong in following Chappell's view both as regards the composer of the melody and the date. He says that John

Stafford Smith included the tune in his Fifth Book of Canzonets, published between 1780 and 1790, and that Smith "probably" composed it about the year 1771.

Let me here definitely state that Smith himself never claimed the tune as his, although he lived after the tune had been sung for thirty years, and even after Key had adapted "The Star-Spangled Banner" to "Anacreon in Heaven." It is simply amazing how one writer blindly copies another without taking pains to verify facts. Mr. Sonneck complacently followed the statement made by Chappell as to the music of "Anacreon in Heaven."

The song was known in 1771, and at that date Smith had composed nothing. He was born in 1750, and studied under Dr. Boyce. His first efforts were a catch and a canon in 1773. The earliest appearance in print of the song was in 1771, and it was included in a song-book called "The Vocal Magazine; or, Compleat British Songster," in 1778. Two years later the music and words were printed by Anne Lee, of Dublin; and they were reprinted in the Vocal Enchantress in 1783.

In order to bolster up Stafford Smith's claim as a composer of the tune, Chappell and his copyists give the date of his Fifth Book of Canzonets as "1780 or 1785." Fortunately for historical accuracy, a wealthy Irish-American, Mr. John Henry Blake, went to the Copyright Office, Stationers' Hall, London, and searched the record indexes of the copyright department from 1746 to 1799, inclusively, with the result that he discovered the actual date on which Smith entered the copyright, namely, May 14, 1799. This was not the only discovery made by Mr. Blake. He also found indisputable evidence that Smith merely *arranged* the tune in the form of a "glee," and that he did not claim any copyright for the tune. Nay, more: Smith lived till the year 1836, and he never asserted his claim as composer of his melody, although Key had written "The Star-Spangled Banner" to it in 1814. Surely it stands to reason that if Smith had composed the tune, and that the said tune (whether set to "Anacreon in Heaven" and "The Star-Spangled Banner") had been sung, printed, and circulated all over the British possessions and in America, he would, as a true Britisher, have asserted his claim to it.

An examination of Smith's Fifth Book of Canzonets reveals not only the interesting fact that this fourth-rate musician merely *arranged* the long-existing melody of "Anacreon," but he also arranged, in a different volume, another Anacreontic song, and likewise "God save the King," and had the audacity to assert that "the whole was *composed* by John Stafford Smith about the year 1780."

Smith's claim to the tune of "Anacreon in Heaven" must therefore be rejected. But still the query remains, Who composed it? First, let me note that the words of the Anacreontic song, now replaced by the words of "The Star-Spangled Banner," are of Irish origin and evidently emanated from Ireland about the year 1765. They were slightly altered in 1770, and as such, were printed in 1778, while some further alterations were made in the version published in 1781. The ascription of the words of the song to "Ralph Tomlinson, Esq.," is based solely on the fact that it was sung by that gentleman as president of the Anacreontic Club in London about the year 1771. And it will be of interest to American readers to learn that the song first appeared in an American song-book, The Vocal Companion, printed and published by an Irishman, Mathew Carey, at Philadelphia, in 1796. To the same tune was adapted "Adams and Liberty," by Thomas Payne, in June, 1798, and published in the *American Musical Miscellany* during the same year.

Having thus eliminated the English claim to the tune, I have no hesitation in claiming the tune as of Irish origin. Furthermore, it has all the characteristics of a composition by the famous Turlough O'Carolan, as can easily be tested by a comparison of "Anacreon" with O'Carolan's "Bumpers, Squire Jones." As O'Carolan died on March 25, 1738, the tune may be dated from about the year 1730, if not earlier. His fine melody known as the "Arethusa" was appropriated by the English, and was included for over a century as a "fine old English melody," until I disproved the ascription and showed its rightful provenance.

It is not a little remarkable that the tune "Yankee Doodle" is also of Irish origin—a fact which I first pointed out in the *Dolphin* in 1905. I now assert that the tune of "The Star-Spangled Banner" is Irish, and is most probably the work of Turlough O'Carolan.

I feel sure that Mr. Sonneck, if a future edition of his official report is called for, will reject the English claim to the tune of "The Star-Spangled Banner" and will admit that of O'Carolan.

Whatever the merits of Mr. Grattan Flood's contentions may be, no reader can fail to notice how boldly and assertively his article of 1912 contradicts his article of 1908 (1909) in almost all essential points, just as if Mr. Grattan Flood in 1912 had completely forgotten what he had written in 1908 (1909). In 1908 (1909), for instance, Mr. Grattan Flood, after confidently stating that the melody of "To Anacreon in Heaven" "was composed by John Stafford Smith, a pupil of Dr. Boyee, in 1771," did not hesitate to say:

> *Internal evidence clearly points to the influence of Boyce*, under whom he was then studying, and some of the phrases are *strongly reminiscent of Boyce's "Heart of Oak*,"

but in 1912 Mr. Grattan Flood, turning his back on his article of 1909 with the asserted English characteristics of the tune, wrote:

> Having thus *eliminated the English claim* to the tune, *I have no hesitation in claiming the tune as of Irish origin.* Furthermore, it has all the characteristics of a composition by the famous O'Carolan, as can easily be tested by a comparison of "Anacreon" with O'Carolan's "Bumpers, Squire Jones." As O'Carolan died on March 25, 1738, the tune may be dated from about the year 1730, if not earlier. . . . I now assert that the tune of "The Star-Spangled Banner" is Irish and is most probably the work of Turlough O'Carolan.

Contradictions like these unfortunately can not but undermine the layman's respect for expert opinion in matters of musical history!

The article of 1912 was bound to be subjected, sooner or later, to the acid test of historical criticism. This ungrateful task was undertaken recently by Rev. H. T. Henry in the Records of the American Catholic Historical Society, December, 1913 (vol. 23, p. 289–335), in a brilliant article headed "The air of the Star-Spangled Banner." With the dialectic technique of the trained theologian Father Henry reaches practically the same historical conclusions as I had reached simultaneously with the argumentative technique of the bibliographer. Father Henry, incorporating some of my own arguments with which he felt himself in accord, sums up more or less the whole controversy. For this reason, consideration of his article, so far as consideration will still be necessary, shall be deferred until the previous literature on the subject has been reported. Father Henry hoped to show—and few, if any of his readers, will deny his success—that (I am quoting his words).

1. The article in the Ave Maria is misleading both in its assertions and in its omissions.

2. "Anacreon" has hardly any characteristic resemblance to "Bumper."

3. The words were most probably composed by Tomlinson; the tune by Smith.

4. Mr. Sonneck's singularly careful "Report" to Congress is completely misrepresented in Dr. Flood's article.

5. There is no evidence, or even what purports to be such, that the tune is Irish in origin, or that the words "emanated from Ireland about the year 1765." In brief, there is no real basis for Dr. Flood's claim.

It is noteworthy that Father Henry, while tearing to shreds Mr. Grattan Flood's tissue of fact and fancy, did so with a sense of charitable humor and without undue harshness or sarcasm.

In the "Report" of 1909 I said, after enumeration of some sources in which "To Anacreon in Heaven" appeared in print:

The inference to be drawn from the insertion of "To Anacreon in Heaven" in the quoted collections, not to mention many later collections, is plain. As those collections were among the most important and most popular of the time, "To Anacreon in Heaven" must have been familiar to all convivial souls in the British Isles toward 1800. Now it is a fact that with the possible exception of that mysterious sheet song of 1771, not one of these publications alludes to the composer of the tune. It was not the rule to do so in miscellaneous collections, yet it is a curious fact that, while contrary to custom, Stewart's Vocal Magazine, 1797, mentions in a separate index the composers of many of the airs, it leaves "To Anacreon in Heaven" without a composer. Possibly the editor doubted the now generally accepted authorship of John Stafford Smith, or he was still unaware of the peculiar form of entry (mentioned by Wm. Chappell as early as 1873!) of "To Anacreon in Heaven" in—

The [*recte A*] fifth book of canzonets, catches, canons & glees, sprightly and plaintive with a part for the piano-forte subjoined where necessary to melodize the score; dedicated by permission to Viscount Dudley and Ward, by John Stafford Smith, Gent. of His Majesty's Chapels Royal, author of the favorite glees, Blest pair of Syrens, Hark the hollow woods, etc. The anacreontic, and other popular songs. Printed for the author. . . .

This collection was published between 1780 and 1790, the exact date being unknown. "To Anacreon in Heaven" appears on page 33, as reproduced here in facsimile. (Appendix, Plate I.) The words "harmonized by the author" may of course mean harmonized by the author of the collection and do not necessarily mean harmonized by the author of the air, but these words, together with the fact that the collection contains none but Smith's own glees, etc., and the wording of the title renders it probable that Smith refers to himself as the composer of the music. But why the words "*harmonized* by the author?" If one looks at the song in its garb as a glee, the bass starting out full of confidence, and the other voices continuing the melody and juggling with it, one is almost apt to see in this peculiar cooperation of the high and low male voices a plausible explanation of the notoriously wide range of "The Star-Spangled Banner," if sung by one voice. This explanation is possible only if the form of "To Anacreon in Heaven" in Smith's Fifth Book was the original form. That we do not know, yet the word "harmonized" renders it improbable. Furthermore, if that was the original form of the piece, then some very radical melodic changes must have taken place in the melody shortly afterwards, as a comparison of the two facsimiles will show. Probably Smith composed it, if he really did compose the tune, as a song for one voice, and in "harmonizing" it for several and different voices he felt obliged to wander away from the original. Of course, if the supposed 1771 sheet song was a sheet song for one voice, and if it contained Smith's name as composer, then all doubt as to original form and to the composer vanishes. We would still have a very simple explanation for the extensive range of the tune. Such a wide range was then (and still is, for that matter) considered the sine qua non of effective drinking songs. Two fine examples, "Anacreon a poet of excellent skill" and "Ye mortals whom trouble & sorrow attend," may be found in the "Anacreontic Songs" of the very conductor of the Anacreontic Society, namely, Dr. Arnold, and, after all, it should not be forgotten that John Stafford Smith could not possibly foresee that his anacreontic masterpiece would some day have to be sung by old and young of an entire nation.

[Foot note.] John Stafford Smith was born, 1750, at Gloucester [Brown and Stratton in British Musical Biography, 1897, say "born at Gloucester about March, 1750." The Gloucester Cathedral Registers (searched for the Library of Congress, 1913) show that he was baptized March 30, 1750. The day of birth is still unknown] and he died at London September 3, 1836. His principal teacher was Dr. Boyce. He became an "able organist, an efficient tenor singer, an excellent composer, and an accomplished antiquary." From 1773 on he won many prizes of the Catch Club for catches, glees, etc., and his five books of glees contain, in the words of Grove, "compositions which place him in the foremost rank of English composers." His famous "Musica Antiqua" appeared in 1812, containing a selection of music "from the 12th to the beginning of the 18th century," for which simple reason it would be futile to look for "To Anacreon in Heaven" in Musica Antiqua.

For certain reasons, the title of Smith's Fifth Book, has been quoted above with the same typographical error "Hark the hollow woods, etc. The Anacreontic" as in the "Report" of 1909 instead of "Hark the hollow woods, etc. the Anacreontic." A reduced facsimile of the correct and complete title will be found in the Appendix as Plate II.

Furthermore, the date of Smith's death, given as above in the "Report" of 1909, appears to be incorrect. Mr. William H. Husk in the old edition of Grove's Dictionary, 1883, had September 20, 1836, but in the new edition of 1908 he has September 21, 1836, as have Brown and Stratton in British Musical Biography, 1897. I have been informed that doubts have been expressed as to the correctness of the year 1836. In view of this doubt, it may not be amiss to quote Mr. Husk (Grove, 1883) to the effect that Smith's will was dated January 21, 1834, and that his widow, Gertrude Stafford Smith, proved the will on October 20, 1836. In addition, the following entertaining bit of gossip will prove incidentally the correctness of the year 1836. Says The Musical World, London, October 14, 1836 (vol. 3, No. 31, p 78), after having stated in No. 30, October 7, that in their last supplement [John] Stafford Smith, Gentleman of His Majesty's Chapels Royal, etc., had been included "among the deceased musicians," whereas he "did not die till the Wednesday succeeding:"

This gentleman was buried at Chelsea, and (from a whim of posthumous vanity) in his full court dress, of a blue silk coat, white satin breeches, waistcoat to correspond, pumps and silver buckles, rings on his fingers, with his goldheaded cane in his hand. . . .

In the number of October 28, 1836, John Roberts indignantly stated that he saw the corpse of his "late valued friend, Mr. Stafford Smith, put into the coffin," and that he vouched "for the falsehood (from beginning to end) of the article on October 14" respecting the dress it was in.

It is safe to say that Mr. Grattan Flood would never have written his article of 1912 without the stimulating perusal of one of the most curious pamphlets that ever came to my notice during a somewhat extensive association with books on music. The complete pamphlet (in folio) bears the title:

> American National Anthem 'Star Spangled Banner.' Made 'Singable' for the voices of the people. History of the origin of the words and music written for the information and use of the American people with modern music setting for all voices and all instruments. Dedicated to the officers and men of the American Army and the officers and men of the American Navy by John Henry Blake . . . Published by John Henry Blake, 503 Fifth Avenue, New York, America, 1912.

As a matter of fact this is merely a 1912 title-page added to a composite pamphlet, the body of which (pp. 2–6) consists of a "History of the origin of the American National Anthem, Brought up to November, 1910" and published with the claim of "Copyright, 1910, by John Henry Blake," no such claim appearing in the records of the United States Copyright Office. Even the body of the pamphlet is a composite affair, inasmuch as the several sections of this history were written at slightly different dates. Mr. Blake submits them to his readers in their chronological order without having kneaded them into a homogeneous whole and it is this more or less disjointed method of presentation which makes the attempt so difficult to "report" the pamphlet briefly or to cope with the discoveries, theories, idiosyncracies, and contradictions therein contained. However, and under the circumstances, no escape is possible from an attempt to do the pamphlet justice *pro et contra*, but we need not concern ourselves here with Mr. Blake's effort to make "The Star-Spangled Banner" more "singable," nor with his conception of the origin of "God save the King," nor with his personal career, nor with any other matter touched upon by Mr. Blake, unless it has an unquestionable and direct bearing on the history of "The Star-Spangled Banner." Furthermore, consideration of the pamphlet must be restricted, so far as possible, to Mr. Blake's own contributions to the subject. It will be seen that much less space is needed to analyze, accept, or reject his theories than to "report" them.

Mr. Blake starts his argument with the statement that the date 1778 of the first edition of the

> Vocal Magazine is the Mason and Dixon dead line of the whole controversy, as it fixes absolutely the exact date when the song first appeared in print.

Nevertheless, after mentioning the reappearance of the song in the Vocal Enchantress of 1783 and other songsters, and disposing of the RoSewig publication of 1909, with the date "Anno 1780," etc., added to his version of the Anne Lee, Dublin, sheet-song edition of "To Anacreon in Heaven" as an "unintentional forgery"; and as a "dangerous derelict" that "should be dynamited," he says that this Anne Lee edition

> is the oldest copy in the British Museum, its date being between 1776 and 1781, and is so acknowledged by such eminent authorities as W. H. Grattan Flood . . . and Frank Kidson.

This contradiction is followed a few lines later by two paragraphs, which must be quoted verbatim:

> As the words of the Song appeared in a bound volume or book, The Vocal Magazine, in 1778, it is reasonable to suppose that it existed as sheet music at least two years before. This is how Kidson attaches his date of 1776 to the Anne Lee, Dublin copy. Naturally it may have existed in *manuscript* many years before.
> That the words already existed in 1778 is shown by the paraphrasing from the *standard words* by Tomlinson in the Vocal Magazine, Leeds Library, Song 566. The second verse, seventh line, is altered to "a fig for Parnassus to Rowley's we'll fly," and in the third verse, second line, changed thus, "To the hill of old Lud will Incontinent flee." This wording changes the scene to London. It is such a flagrant piece of paraphrasing that it proves that the song already existed. It also casts a cloud on Tomlinson's claim to the composition of the original words. Kidson has recently got wise to this situation. However, we have no interest in the old words except as an aid to trace the composer of the Music.

The reader will not have failed to notice that the claim of "a flagrant piece of paraphrasing" of the text as it stands in the Vocal Magazine, 1778,[a] is based on the assumption that the date of the undated Anne Lee edition is two years earlier, namely, 1776, and on the fact, which Mr. Blake forgot to make clear, that the text of the Anne Lee edition differs from the text in the Vocal Magazine, 1778, in this, that it contains no reference "to the hill of old Lud" (Ludgate Hill) in London.

Mr. Blake's next step is what he terms the "explosion and complete annihilation of the theory that John Stafford Smith . . .

---

[a] Mr. Blake says: "There were three editions of it—1778, 1779, and 1781. The British Museum has only the 1781 edition, but the Public Library at Leeds has the edition of 1778." So has the Library of Congress. In his letter of November 24, 1913, Mr. Frank Kidson informs me: "I have never seen or heard of a 1779 edition of the Vocal Magazine except that in Sir J. Stainer's 'Catalogue of Song books' he mentions that besides this 1781 edition, which he has, there were ones for 1778 and 1779." It will interest bibliographers to learn that the Library of Congress recently acquired a London, Harrison and Co., *1784* edition, contents identical with those of the 1778 ed., except that it has no preface.

composed the music of "Anacreon in Heaven." He takes this step by adding to a quotation from Chappell's Notes and Queries article (1873) the following "comment:"

> In October, 1910, we diligently searched the record indexes of the Copyright Department in Stationer's Hall, London, from the year 1746 to the year 1799, both inclusive, and found only the Copyright Claim of this "Fifth Book of Canzonets, Catches, &c." which contains on page 33 the **Glee** taken from "The Anacreontic Song," Author, John Stafford Smith—entered May 8, 1799. See Official Certificate below of Stationer's Hall dated October 20, 1910.
>
> We will gladly pay anyone who can find any entry of copyright of the Song "Anacreon in Heaven," two pounds for an official certificate of such entry, for their time in looking up the records. We can find no copyright of it anywhere in Stationer's Hall. . . .
>
> Mr. Chappell might have gone down to Stationer's Hall himself, or sent a boy, as he had a score of employees. We are sorry to be obliged to cause the Music Publishers so much trouble, but thirty-seven years is a long interval in which no one had sufficient enterprise to consult the copyright office at Stationer's Hall. The date, 1799, completely eliminates J. W. [!] Smith as *original* composer. He claimed for a copyright on the "Anacreontic Song" arranged as a *Glee* only. On page 33 it is arranged as a *Glee* for *three voices*. And he takes particular trouble to *disclaim* original Authorship, not only in the *Index*, but also at top of the Music on page 33 by stating, "*Harmonized by the Author.*" The music and words of the *Glee* are a "high old mix." The Music Dictionary definition of "Glee" is "a secular composition for three or more unaccompanied solo voices peculiar to England."
>
> Chappell being a skilled musician ought to have said, "The Anacreontic Song" arranged as a "Glee"—his omission has made a whole lot of trouble. Smith's compositions consisted almost entirely of Glees [!?]. This evidence not only eliminates J. W. [!] Smith, but opens up the composition to the world, with a probability of its being Irish or French, or possibly American.

Not satisfied with his discovery of the date of copyright of Smith's Fifth Book—a discovery for which Mr. Blake deserves fullest credit, since it involved a good deal of patience—Mr. Blake procured a certified copy of the original entry from the Registrar of the Copyright Office at Stationers' Hall. It appears that on May 8, 1799, copyright entry was made for—

> A Fifth Book . . . [for complete title *compare* Appendix, Plate II] . . . dedicated . . . by John Stafford Smith . . . Author of the favourite glees, Blest pair of Syrens, Hark the Hollow Woods, etc., The Anacreontic, and other popular Songs. [N. B. the comma before The with its capital T]

Under "*Property of*" we read "*Author,*" under "*Share*" we read "*Whole,*" and the "Certificate [was] given May 14th, 1799."

Mr. Blake then quotes from his "rapid-fire correspondence" with Mr. Kidson, who, on October 23, 1910, wrote:

> I don't see that this entry in the least alters the contention that John Stafford Smith composed the air "To Anacreon in Heaven" long before he published his Fifth Book of Conzonets.
>
> On the title page of this book he definitely states that he is the "author" (meaning composer) of certain works, including "The Anacreontic, and other popular

songs," and on page 33 he states that it is "harmonized by the author," thus again claiming the air *which he now alters into a Glee.* All this is quite probable, and until you can make him out a deliberate liar you have to accept his very reasonable statement.

Again you say that you believe that Ralph Tomlinson did not write the words, but paraphrased them. I can not see any grounds for this belief in face of the fact that Tomlinson's name as author of the words is attached to dozens of contemporary copies. . .

From a previous letter by Mr. Kidson (Oct. 21, 1910) the following sentence must be quoted in justice to Mr. Kidson, as it gives his views of the date of the Anne Lee edition of "To Anacreon in Heaven:"

Words and Music on a Sheet Song by Anne Lee, Dublin, *after* February 1776 (when her husband died and she took the business and before 1788 when she gave up the business).

To this sentence Mr. Blake added in parenthesis "Granted by Blake."

Mr. Blake's comment on the Kidson letter of October 23 was:

The above is a very nice letter, but a copyright certificate stating he is the Author (not composer) holds good in a court of law, and is a very stubborn fact. The "Glee" copyright entry of May 8th, 1799, absolutely disposes of Chappell's claim for J. S. Smith.

It is here not yet the place to show that a "glee" copyright by no means "annihilates" the possibility that the claimant many years previously had been the author, *id est,* composer of the air (theme) of the glee in form of a song for one voice and chorus refrain, which song he or the original publisher neglected to enter at Stationers' Hall for copyright.

Mr. Blake then informs us that he sent to the United States War and Navy Departments photographs of the title page of the Fifth Book, "One of the *Glee,* page 33," of the Fifth Book, one of the Anne Lee, Dublin, edition of "To Anacreon in Heaven" (reproduced in facsimile in Appendix, Plate III, by permission of the Navy Department), and "One of the Song, To Anacreon in Heaven, by E. Rhames, Dublin, who, Kidson says, published from 1775 to 1790. This Rhames copy was obtained through the courtesy of W. H. Grattan Flood, and may be as early as 1775." (Also reproduced in facsimile in Appendix, Plate IV, by permission of the Navy Department.)

How utterly impossible this date "as early as 1775" is, will be seen subsequently. It will also be seen how this impossibility eliminates all implied deductions from so early a date as to the authorship of the text, the "flagrant paraphrasing" the text, etc.

Mr. Blake continues by saying:

Had Smith claimed composition for the original music of this Song, "To Anacreon in Heaven," he would probably have invalided his Glee copyright. We judge Smith was a good business man. The words of "To Anacreon in Heaven" appeared in the 1778 edition of the Vocal Magazine, and Smith claimed for his *Glee* in 1799, or twenty-one years afterwards. In the meantime scores [!?] of publishers in Ireland, Scotland, America and England published perhaps a million [!??] copies of the song, and gave the honor of the composition to no man. And Smith, although he lived till 1836, never claimed that honor, but on the contrary he disclaimed the honor in order to get copyright on his "Glee."

We repeat that there is a probability of the origin of the music being Irish or French, or possibly American.

Francis Scott Key produced "The Star-Spangled Banner" in 1814, and Smith lived for twenty-two years afterwards and never claimed the Music! Smith never had the reputation of being a philanthropist, yet the royalties on the original composition would have made him a millionaire [!??] in those days!

Discounting Mr. Blake's rather fantastic estimate of eighteenth century royalties, etc., an attentive reader will immediately ask: "Even if John Stafford Smith were annihilated as composer of 'To Anacreon in Heaven' would that really destroy the possibility that nevertheless the air was of *English* origin? Why would the elimination of just *one English* composer eliminate *all other English* composers and argue eo ipso for the probability of the music being Irish or French or possibly American"? To these very natural questions Mr. Blake ventures no reply. Probably they never occurred to him in his strenuous effort to remove from the music of "The Star-Spangled Banner" the (to his eyes offensive) stain of a "monarchical" English origin.

However, according to Mr. Blake, it is "all a mistake in punctuation." He says:

> William Chappell, Frank Kidson, The Library of Congress (see page 22, where the error is very pronounced), all fell into the same punctuation trap and never discovered it. In the Transcription of the Title Page of Smith's Fifth Book, &c., they all say when it comes to the point or "real target" "The Anacreontic" commencing the word "the" before Anacreontic with a capital "T," and putting a period before the word, and thus commencing an entirely new sentence and thus throwing the Anacreontic out of the *Glees*. (Kidson admits it is a *"Glee."*)
>
> In the engraved title page it is a small "t," and the period belongs to the abbreviated "&c."—continuing on the same sentence and retaining the Anacreontic among the Glees. Look at and compare the Title page photograph sent herewith. It changes the whole meaning. We discovered this about the first time we looked at the *real* title page, but no one would believe it unless backed up by the testimony of the photograph of the Title Page, by the photograph of the Glee on page 33, and the certificate of Copyright in 1799, and we had a bad three weeks finding that Copyright record. *Compare the photograph.*

Mr. Blake correctly noticed in my "Report" of 1909 the typographical error described above, but the reader is warned not to accept Mr. Blake's grammatical deductions therefrom before these deductions have been scrutinized.

The same warning applies to Mr. Blake's half sarcastic:

> Discovery that Smith wrote two "Anacreontic" glees, one in the year 1780 and the other in the year 1799, and also the British anthem "God Save the King."

This line of attack is based on Mr. Blake's acquisition of another well-known collection of music by John Stafford Smith. A copy of this is in the Library of Congress, which possesses more "books bearing on the American National Anthem, or relating and appertaining thereto" than Mr. Blake would have his readers believe in the face of certain quotations and facsimiles from such books in my "Report" of 1909 which was known and used by Mr. Blake. In fairness to Mr. Blake, but also in fairness to John Stafford Smith, Mr. Blake's entire argument, divested of irrelevant embroidery, must here be quoted at the risk of swelling this chapter to inordinate length. Mr. Blake writes:

A Miscellaneous Collection of New Songs, Catches, and Glees for one, two, three, four, and five Voices, particularly an Occasional Ode Song after Dinner at the Pantheon, which gained the Premium this year, and a Cantata entitled "The Frantic Lady." The whole composed by John Stafford Smith, London, Printed and Sold by James Blundell, Music Seller to his Royal Highness, The Duke of Cumberland, No. 10, Hay Market, facing the Opera House.

Size page 9½ x 13½ oblong . 51 pages . all complete. (Please note there is no punctuation error here, and that Smith "claims" the *whole!*)

INDEX.

On page 2. *"The Occasional Ode for 1780,* which gained a Premium." This fixes absolutely the date of the book and Ode, *1780.* The Ode occupies eleven pages of music and words, and is remarkably well printed.

Commencing on page 35 under title *Anacreontic* is a *glee* occupying seven pages of words and music. The words commence "Is it Summer?" The words and music bear not the slightest resemblance to the song "To Anacreon in Heaven," but Smith calls it *"Anacreontic"* in large type and by that one word only. It does not bear the slightest resemblance to the music of the "Star Spangled Banner."

This enables our esteemed opponents, Chappell, Kidson, and Groves' Dictionary to retire in good order on their *"Claim"* that Smith wrote an *Anacreontic* in *1780.* They all were merely "barking up the wrong tree."

On Page 27. *A Canon* in Subdiapente, 2 in (one), on a plain Song.

The peculiarity of the heading caught our eye, and we must admit that the phrase is entirely too technical for our limited vocabulary. We noticed it was a Glee for three voices. Then we read the words "Si Deus pro nobis, quis contra nos," repeated ad libitum by the *first* and *third* voices. Then we were electrified to find the intermediate *second* voice roaring gloriously away on our old familiar friend in the King's own English, "God Save Great George our King, long live our noble King, God Save the King, God Save the King." The music is practically that of Dr. John Bull, and quite the same as the Music is sung to-day. And this in the year *1780,* of which the date is absolutely fixed by the title page and *1780* in bold type on page 2 and on page 34, *"Round for 1780,"* which is directly opposite the *Anacreontic,* page 35.

Verily this man Smith was a Wonder—he was determined to get on record in the National Anthem of America whichever of the two is finally chosen.

He composed a "Glee" on "God Save the King" 175 years after the original music was written by Dr. John Bull. He composed a "Glee" on "To Anacreon in Heaven" 21 years after that *Mystery* appeared in print in 1778. In the year 1780 he published a book of his compositions, one of which was an "*Anacreontic*," yet all his long life of 86 years he never claimed composition of "To Anacreon in Heaven."

However, his English friends save him the trouble, and consequently "*claim*" he was the composer of the original music of "The Star Spangled Banner," and also of "God Save the King." They say read his *title pages*. Yes, read them!! "They are hoist with their own petard!" It is not necessary to descend to vulgarity, but simply to say that Smith confined himself to the deliberate legal truth!!!

Mr. Blake will not take offense, it is hoped, if his "Annual Supplement, November, 1911," on page 7 of his pamphlet, is not here reported, since it is wholly irrelevant and since it deals with Mr. Blake's personal affairs just as lively and naively as with the poet Anacreon. This supplement is preceded by a section headed "In conclusion," from which the following is quoted:

We have now produced evidence that we believe would prove to any Army or Navy Board that "Music composed in his Majestie's Chapels Royal by John Stafford Smith" (see Library of Congress Report, page 22) does not belong on "The Star Spangled Banner," and as an American citizen we demand it be taken off, and believe that some Members of Congress will help to take it off. The wording is too *Monarchical* for Americans. What is the use of having the Munroe Doctrine and leaving a Monarchical Claim on our National Anthem.

Who composed the Music of Anacreon in Heaven? We do not know. No one knows; it is a *Mystery*. No one has dared to claim the Music, not in one hundred and forty years. . . .

It may be Irish, for why all these pre-historic beautifully printed and complete standard copies from Dublin. Of course the Anne Lee Copy in the British Museum is "claimed" to be the oldest, perhaps because it says "Sung in London," but *is it older* than the Lizzie Rhames copy, equally as well printed (photographs of both enclosed) which says nothing about London, and naturally cannot be found in the British Museum? . . .

It may be French, for the Anne Lee Copy is bound up with a lot of French Songs, and part French and English word songs, published by the same Lee family, and at about the same date, and the very first time it appeared in America under the verified date of 1797 it was set to the words "The Genius of France from his Star begemmed throne," meaning Napoleon, and in honor of the French Independence Day, July 14th. . . ."

It may be American, for did not an American "claim" it for us in 1896? There was an Anacreontic Society in New York in 1795.

In our humble opinion the Music has come down through the ages, probably through the Troubadours, for it has always been a Song for men, and no one but an opera singer of the "premier etoile" quality can negotiate it. Even English or Irish voices of to-day cannot do it justice.

It may have been composed by Richard Coeur de Lion, who as a Troubadour could compose and sing a good song, and as a Crusader could swing a mighty battle-axe in the Cause of Christianity. Perhaps it was the very song that led to his release when made a captive by the King of Germany, on his return journey from the Crusades and immured for a year in a castle in an obscure village. . . .

It requires voices produced only in that climate where the sunlit valleys of Southern France and the plains of Northern Italy meet, to sing it with justice, and "admiration." That climate which produces voices that draw a salary equal to a small fortune each night they sing.

Somewhere in some old forgotten manuscript, in some Library, or Monastery, or Antiquary Shop, the Original Music may be revealed; as was "God Save the King" after two hundred years; a disputation of another hundred years more will probably follow.

The discovery of an authentic original manuscript of "To Anacreon in Heaven" with the composer's autograph signature, or even of a contemporary publication of the song with the composer's name, would perhaps settle this whole controversy indeed, and, to the relief of all concerned, would relegate the efforts of historians to establish the composer from circumstantial evidence to the shelves of oblivion. On the other hand, it is to be feared that musical history can not be written with anachronistic imagination, such as Mr. Blake displays. If a musical scholar, fairly expert in "stilkritische" distinctions and not familiar with the controversy here under discussion, were asked to date the anonymous "To Anacreon in Heaven," his answer perhaps would read:

The melody of "To Anacreon in Heaven" with its unusual demands of range of voice is hardly that of a folk-song. Unless the words were fitted to an existing melody, the impression is prompted that the melody was composed for the effective display of a voice of wide range, either of the composer himself or in anticipation of some other singer of reliable ability. The structure of the melody suggests the homophonic period. The "Anacreontic" text points to the wave of taste that was still at its height toward the end of the eighteenth century with countless "Anacreontic" songs inspired by the philosophy of life of the poet Anacreon. Barring conflicting evidence, the melody, therefore, may be said to perhaps have had its origin during the last quarter of the eighteenth century. Its characteristic quality is a stately, enthusiastic, and youthful optimism, well suited to official convivial purposes of an Anacreontic society. It may be that the melody appealed so strongly to the traditionally optimistic people of the United States exactly because of its optimistic atmosphere.

Disregarding minor matters, the main and troublesome question appears to be: Did or did not John Stafford Smith compose "To Anacreon in Heaven"? As was stated above, his name does not seem to appear in any of the eighteenth century publications of the song except in his own Fifth Book. As against Chappell's plausible interpretation of this fact in favor of Smith's authorship, Mr. Blake argues an "annihilation" of the claim put up for Smith from the very same Fifth Book! Let us see if perhaps an investigation of the history of "The Anacreontic Society" will lead to a firm and clear path out of the jungle of claims and counterclaims.

In his Musical Memoirs (1830, Vol. I, pp. 80–84) W. T. Parke entered under the year 1786 these entertaining lines:

> This season I became an honorary member of the Anacreontic Society, and at the first meeting played a concerto on the oboe, as did Cramer on the violin. The assemblage of subscribers was as usual very numerous, amongst whom were several noblemen and gentlemen of the first distinction. Sir Richard Hankey (the banker) was the chairman. This fashionable society consisted of a limited number of members, each of whom had the privilege of introducing a friend, for which he paid in his subscription accordingly. The meetings were held in the great ballroom of the Crown and Anchor Tavern in the Strand, once a fortnight during the season, and the entertainments of the evening consisted of a grand concert, in which all the flower of the musical profession assisted as honorary members. After the concert an elegant supper was served up; and when the cloth was removed, the constitutional song, beginning, "To Anacreon in Heaven," was sung by the chairman or his deputy. This was followed by songs in all the varied styles, by theatrical singers and the members, and catches and glees were given by some of the first vocalists in the kingdom. The late chairman, Mr. Mulso, possessed a good tenor voice, and sang the song alluded to with great effect . . .
>
> This society, to become members of which noblemen and gentlemen would wait a year for a vacancy, was by an act of gallantry brought to a premature dissolution. The Duchess of Devonshire, the great leader of the *haut ton*, having heard the Anacreontic highly extolled, expressed a particular wish to some of its members to be permitted to be privately present to hear the concert, &c., which being made known to the directors, they caused the elevated orchestra occupied by the musicians at balls to be fitted up, with a lattice affixed to the front of it, for the accommodation of her grace and party, so that they could see, without being seen; but some of the comic songs, not being exactly calculated for the entertainment of ladies, the singers were restrained; which displeasing many of the members, they resigned one after another; and a general meeting being called, the society was dissolved.

Misreading slightly Mr. Parke's reminiscences, C[harles] M.[ackeson] in Grove's Dictionary claimed that Parke wrote of the dissolution of the club in 1786, which he, of course, did not do. Nor would the year 1786 be tenable, since Pohl in his scholarly book on "Mozart and Haydn in London," 1867 (v. 2, p. 107), gleaned from the Gazetteer of January 14, 1791, that Haydn was the guest of honor at the society's concert on January 12. Nor is Mr. Grattan Flood correct if he, in his "Notes on the Origin of 'To Anacreon in Heaven,'" sent me in June, 1908, dates the dissolution of the society 1796. The "Musical Directory for the Year 1794" in the "List of various musical societies" states distinctly: "The Anacreontic Society which *met* at the Crown and Anchor Tavern in the Strand, the festivities of which *were* heightened by a very Select Band." Consequently the society no longer existed in 1794.[a] This is not at all contradicted by the entry under Dr. Samuel Arnold "Conductor at Acad[emy of Ancient Music], Ana[creontic Society]," because the title-page distinctly reads "musical societies of which they [the professors of music] are *or have been* members." (To avoid confusion it may here be added that "To Anacreon in Heaven" is not contained in the "Anacreontic Songs for 1, 2, 3, & 4 voices composed and selected by Dr. Arnold and dedicated by permission to the Anacreontic Society," London, J. Bland, 1785. The absence from this book is a strong argument against Arnold's authorship of "To Anacreon in Heaven.")

In the seventh edition of the first part of "The Festival of Anacreon. Containing a collection of modern songs, written for the Anacreontic Society, the Beef-Steak, and Humbug Clubs. By Captain Morris, Mr. Brownlow [etc.], London, George Peacock, n. d." there appears on pages 80–83 the text of "To Anacreon, in Heaven," headed as "Song. Sung by Mr. Bannister, at the Anacreontic Society" and on pages 6–7 this

"SHORT ACCOUNT OF THE ANACREONTIC SOCIETY.

In the infant state of this admirable institution, the members met as they now do, once a fortnight, during the winter season, at the London Coffee-house, on Ludgate-hill, who were chiefly of the sprightly class of citizens; but the popularity of the club soon increased the number of its members, and it was found expedient to remove the meeting to a place where the members could be more commodiously accommodated; the Crown and Anchor in the Strand was accordingly fixed on, where this meeting has ever since been held.

---

[a] This conjecture is not necessarily contradicted by "The Ugly Club: a dramatic caricature in one act. Performed on the 6th of June, 1798, at the Theatre Royal, Drury-Lane . . . By Edmund Spenser, the younger," London, Printed and published for the author, 1798. (40 p. 21½ cm. Library of Congress, Longe collection, vol. 273.) This piece winds up with:

SONG.

To the lame old Gold-smith, who was wiv'd from the sea,
  The Sons of Deformity sent a petition,
That he their inspirer and patron would be:—
  Soon this answer arrived from rickety Vulcan,
  'To the call I attend,
  Quick from heaven descend,
  Frolic Pan with his cittern I'll bring in my hand.
Repeated shouts of loud mirth the world shall apprise,
That men may be happy without nose, feet, or eyes.'

Follow five more stanzas of this obvious parody of 'To Anacreon in Heaven' and in last stanza at first line "Come, Sons of Deformity, let's join hand in hand " occurs this footnote:
"The Club rise, as is customary in the Anacreontic Society, and join hands."
Either, then, the society still existed when this play was written (which might have been years before 1798) or the author did not know of its dissolution.

ANACREON, the renown'd convivial Bard of ancient Greece, as distinguished for the delicacy of his wit, as he is for the easy, elegant and natural turn of his poesy, is the character from which this society derives its title, and who has been happily celebrated in the Constitutional Song, beginning, 'To Anacreon, in heaven,' &c. universally acknowledged to be a very classical, poetic, and well-adapted composition; and if our information does not mislead us, it was written by a gentleman of the Temple, now dead, whose name was Tomlinson, and originally sung by Mr. Webster, and afterwards by Charles Bannister, whose secession from the society, in consequence of some frivolous punctilios, is much to be regretted; for to do justice to the song, a very animated execution is requisite: that power of voice, happy discrimination, and vivacity, which seems peculiar to the well-known exertions of Mr. Bannister in this composition, never fail of producing him what he justly merits—*unbounded applause*.

Mr. Hankey, the Banker, a gentleman highly spoken of, as a man of polished manners and most liberal sentiments, now presides at this meeting, by whose management, in conjunction with the other directors, every thing is conducted under the influence of the strictest propriety and decorum.

The Concert, which commences at eight o'clock, and concludes at ten, is entirely composed of professional men in the first class of genius, science, and execution, which the present age can boast of. After the concert is over, the company adjourns to a spacious adjacent apartment, partake of a cold collation, and then return to the concert-room, where the remainder of the evening is totally devoted to wit, harmony, and the God of wine."

Of the exceedingly scarce The Festival of Anacreon, the Library of Congress possesses also the undated sixth edition of the second part. The British Museum lists only a copy of the third part with conjectural date 1810. The evasive first edition of The Festival of Anacreon must have appeared after 1780, because July 16, 1780, is mentioned on page 72 of the first part as date of death of Sir John Moore, the author of "Aylesbury Races. A ballad." Furthermore, during the club season of 1786–87, according to Parke, Sir Richard Hankey was the chairman, evidently the gentleman mentioned in The Festival of Anacreon. Therefore we have 1786–87 as approximate date of publication. Indeed we seem to have good reason for dating the first edition 1788 or 1789, since the two frontispieces in the Library of Congress copy are dated November 8 and October 15, 1788. In that case, Sir Richard Hankey would seem to have succeeded himself in the chair for several seasons.[a]

However, even before Sir Richard's presidency The Anacreontic Society had aroused the interest of magazine writers, including foreigners. As proof I submit in translation what a London correspondent to Cramer's Magazin der Musik, Hamburg, May 9, 1783 (p. 550–551), wrote under date of April, 1783:

Several weeks ago I was invited to a concert . . . It is called the Anacreontic Society and this institution is said to be more than three hundred years old. There was music from 7.30 to 10 o'clock; the invited virtuosos play *gratis*, but in turn hear vocal music for nothing. About ten o'clock we went to another room for supper. During supper, tables and benches were placed in the concert-

---

[a] As against these conjectural dates Lowndes Bibliographer's Manual (1871) has 1783 as date for first part and 1789 as date of its sixth edition.

room and the platform, where the orchestra had been before, was now occupied with vocalists and the tables were supplied with punch, "Bischoff" and wine. This was the arrangement found by us after supper and it was quite a pleasure to hear good songs without accompaniment over a glass of punch. They sang mostly canons and very well indeed. The vocalists, seated at their tables on the platform and mostly amateurs "punschten mit", and the leader announced the toasts. On this institution I hope to procure you detailed information, which probably would be welcome to you.

Unfortunately the correspondent did not do so. At any rate, Cramer's Magazine contains no further reference to "The Anacreontic Society." Between the lines one may read that the London correspondent had his polite doubts about the society being "more than three hundred years old," which would carry us farther back than the discovery of America. Since others may be more credulous than our German correspondent, the following anonymous "History of the Anacreontic Society" addressed to Mr. Urban, the editor of the Gentleman's Magazine, London, and there published in May, 1780, pages 224–225, is here added immediately:

I will not pay you so ill a compliment to suppose you have never heard of the Anacreontic Society. I therefore flatter myself the following account of its institution and progress will not be unacceptable to you or your polite readers.— It was begot and christened by a Mr. S—th (1) [in footnote: Mr. S—th, better known amongst his acquaintances by the familiar appellation of Jack S—th, is a Dog at a Catch, and a corner-stone of Society] about the year 1766, at a genteel public-house near the Mansion-house, was nursed at the Feathers and Half-moon Taverns in Cheapside, and received a great part of its establishment at the London Coffee-house (2) [in footnote: Mr. Bellas, President].

The society at this house consisted of 25 members, and each member admitted his friend. Applications for admittance at this time became so numerous, it was thought necessary to remove the society to a house where the accommodations were more spacious. It was therefore carried to the Crown and Anchor in the Strand (3) [in footnote: Mr. Tomlinson, President], and the number of members increased to 40, with the former indulgence of admitting friends. The year following, ten new members were admitted, and friends introduced the alternate nights only. About two years since (4) [in footnote: Mr. Mulso, President] the number of members were increased to fourscore (5) [in footnote: The present members consist of Peers, Commoners, Aldermen, Gentlemen, Proctors, Actors, and Polite Tradesmen], and each member admits a visitor as before. The subscription at present is three guineas, and to a new member three and a half. The expense to non-subscribers is six shillings. The society opens generally about the middle of November, and their entertainments are on every other Wednesday till the twelve nights are accomplished. The concert, which consists of the best performers (who are honorary members) in London, begins at half past seven, and ends at a quarter before ten. The company then adjourns to another room, where an elegant supper is provided; in the meantime, the grand room is prepared for their return. The tables at the upper end of the room are elevated for the vocal performers. Here conviviality reigns in every shape, catches and glees in their *proper stile*, single songs from the first performers, imitations by gentlemen, much beyond any stage exhibition, salt-box solos, and miniature puppet-shews; in short, every thing that mirth can suggest.

The following classical song, written by poor Ralph Tomlinson, their late president, is chorused by the whole company, and opens the mirth of the evening. [Follows the text of "To Anacreon in Heaven" headed "Anacreontic Song."]

These entertaining accounts of the aims and habits of the "Anacreontic Society" of London [a] will have made it clear that the club generally "opened" about the middle of November and ended its season about the middle of May.   Now, "about two years since" May, 1780—magazines were then generally published at the end not at the beginning of the month—would be about May, 1778.   "Ten new members" had been admitted the year previous, which would be the year 1777.   This happened "the year following" the removal of the "Anacreontic Society" from the "London Coffee House" on Ludgate Hill to the Crown and Anchor Tavern in the Strand during the presidency of Ralph Tomlinson.   In other words, the year of Tomlinson's presidency and of the club's removal from the London Coffee House to the Crown and Anchor seems to have been 1776, either during the club season 1775–76 or 1776–77.   The reader will do well to keep this seemingly insignificant point in mind.

The admittedly earliest known appearance of the text of "To Anacreon in Heaven" occurs in the first edition of "The Vocal Magazine, or, British Songster's Miscellany, containing all the English, Scotch, and Irish Songs, Cantatas, Glees, Catches, Airs, Ballads, etc., deemed any way worthy of being transmitted to posterity.   Volume the first.   London, Printed by J. Harrison for J. Bew, 1778."   The "magazine" is announced in the preface to be "regularly published every month."   This explains why the volume with its 1,286 texts of songs is divided into nine "Numbers," and why the dates of the two copperplates with portraits of vocal performers accompanying each number run from May 1, 1778, to January 1, 1779.   (The volume is entirely without music.   The tunes are not even indicated by title.)   To have compiled this treasure house of texts of fugitive but once more or less popular songs of every description must have taken the editor years, which is another point I request the reader to bear in mind.

In Number IV of this Vocal Magazine, 1778 (compare Appendix, Plate V), the copperplates being dated August 1, 1778, are published on pages 147–148 as Song 566, the words of,

ANACREONTIC SOCIETY.

Written by Ralph Tomlinson, Esq.

To Anacreon, in Heav'n, where he sat in full glee,
    A few sons of harmony sent a petition,
That he their inspirer and patron would be;
    When this answer arriv'd from the jolly old Grecian—
        Voice, fiddle, and flute,
        No longer be mute;
    I'll lend ye my name, and inspire ye to boot:
    And, besides, I'll instruct ye, like me, to intwine
    The myrtle of Venus with Bacchus's vine.

---

[a] The "Anacreontic Society" (1729–1865) of Dublin from the brief allusions in Mr. Wm. H. Grattan Flood's History of Irish Music, Dublin, 1905, appears to have been a musical society of the more customary type.

The news through Olympus immediately flew;
    When old Thunder pretended to give himself airs—
If these mortals are suffer'd their scheme to pursue,
    The devil a goddess will stay above stairs.
        Hark! already they cry,
        In transports of joy,
    A fig for Parnassus! to Rowley's we'll fly;
    And there, my good fellows, we'll learn to intwine
    The myrtle of Venus with Bacchus's vine.

The yellow-hair'd god, and his nine fusty maids,
    To the hill of old Lud will incontinent flee,
Idalia will boast but of tenantless shades,
    And the biforked hill a mere desert will be.
        My thunder, no fear on't,
        Will soon do its errand,
    And, dam'me! I'll swinge the ringleaders, I warrant.
    I'll trim the young dogs, for thus daring to twine
    The myrtle of Venus with Bacchus's vine.

Apollo rose up; and said, Pr'ythee ne'er quarrel,
    Good king of the gods, with my vot'ries below!
Your thunder is useless—then, shewing his laurel,
    Cry'd, *Sic evitabile fulmen*, you know!
        Then over each head
        My laurels I'll spread;
    So my sons from your crackers no mischief shall dread,
    Whilst snug in their club-room, they jovially twine
    The myrtle of Venus with Bacchus's vine.

Next Momus got up, with his risible phiz,
    And swore with Apollo he'd chearfully join—
The full tide of harmony still shall be his,
    But the song, and the catch, and the laugh shall be mine:
        Then, Jove, be not jealous
        Of these honest fellows.
    Cry'd Jove, We relent, since the truth you now tell us;
    And swear, by Old Styx, that they long shall intwine
    The myrtle of Venus with Bacchus's vine.

Ye sons of Anacreon, then, join hand in hand;
    Preserve unanimity, friendship, and love.
'Tis your's to support what's so happily plan'd;
    You've the sanction of gods, and the fiat of Jove.
        While thus we agree,
        Our toast let it be.
    May our club flourish happy, united, and free!
    And long may the sons of Anacreon intwine
    The myrtle of Venus with Bacchus's vine.

These further appearances of the text of "To Anacreon in Heaven,"
with or without music, in eighteenth century magazines and songsters

are known to me.   (Unless acknowledgment of source is made, the books are understood to be in the Library of Congress.)

1780. March, in the London Magazine, p. 134.   Headed "Anacreontick Song. By the late R. Tomlinson."   (Text only.)

1780. May, p. 224–225 in the Gentleman's Magazine, London.   Headed "Anacreontic Song."   (Text only.)

1780. The Bullfinch, London, p. 362, as "Song CCCCLVII.   The Anacreontick Song.   By Ralph Tomlinson, Esq., late President of that Society."   (Text only.   Communication by Mr. Frank Kidson, November 3, and November 24, 1913.)

[1783] The Vocal Enchantress, London, J. Fielding (frontispiece dated 1783), p. 336–337.   Headed simply "Song CLXVII."   (Text and air.   Compare Appendix, Plate VI.)

1785. The Humming Bird or A complete collection of the most esteemed songs . . . Third Edition . . . Canterbury, 1785, p. 300.   (Text only.   No title given to any of the songs.   Communication of Mr. Frank Kidson, November 29, 1913.)

1786. The Musical Miscellany, Perth.   Headed "Song XII To Anacreon in Heaven."   (Communication by Mr. Grattan Flood, December 29, 1909, and Mr. Kidson, November 29, 1913.)

- 1788. Calliope; or The Musical Miscellany, London, C. Elliot and T. Kay, p. 5–7, headed "Song IV, To Anacreon in Heaven."   (Text and air.) [a]

[1788] The festival of Anacreon, London, first part, seventh ed., p. 80–83.   (1788 being the approximate date of the first ed.)   Headed "Song.   Sung by Mr. Bannister, at the Anacreontic Society."   (Text only.)

[1788] The Royalty Songster and Convivial Companion (frontispiece dated 1788), p. 9.   Headed "Anacreontic Song, Sung by Mr. Bannister."   (Text only. Communication of Mr. Frank Kidson, November 3, 1913.)

1789. The New Vocal Enchantress . . . a new edition for 1788.   On p. 289 as "Song; sung by Mr. Sedgwick at the Anacreontic Society."   (Text only. Communication of Mr. Frank Kidson, November 29, 1913.)

[1790] The Busy Bee, vol. II, p. 80.   Headed "LXX.   Sung by Mr. Bannister at the Anacreontic.   Written by Mr. Thomlinson."   (Text only.   Communication by Mr. Frank Kidson, November 3 and November 24, 1913.)

1790. The Billington or Town and Country Songster, p. 311.   Headed "Anacreontic Song.   By Mr. Bannister."   (Text only.   Communication by Mr. Frank Kidson, November 3, 1913.) [b]

1790. The Banquet of Thalia, pref. dated York, 1790.   On p. 85 as "Song.   Anacreontic."   (Text only.   Communication of Mr. Frank Kidson, November 29, 1913.)

1791. September, in the London Magazine and Monthly Chronology, Dublin, Exshaw.   Headed "The Anacreontic Song.   Sung by Mr. Incledon with universal applause."   (Text and music.   Mr. W. J. Lawrence in his article on "Eighteenth-century magazine music," Musical Antiquary, October, 1911.   Facsimile, by permission of the Royal Library, Dublin, see Appendix, Plate VII.)

[a] Of this songster the editor says in a prefatory note: "May properly be considered as a new edition, although under a different title" of the Musical Miscellany (a collection published at Perth in 1786.)

[b] Mr. Kidson adds this entertaining bit of information that on page 314 of the same songster appears, and in the metre of "To Anacreon in Heaven" of which it obviously is a parody: "A new Anacreontic Song.   Sung by Mr. Sedgwick with great applause at the Royalty Theatre," beginning "To banish life's troubles the Grecian old sage."

1792. Edinburgh Musical Miscellany, Vol. I, p. 1–4. Headed "Song I. To Anacreon in Heaven. Sung by Mr. Bannister at the Anacreontic Society."
(Text and air.)

1792. The Banquet of Thalia, pref. dated York, 1792. On p. 85 as "Song Anacreontic." (Text only. Communication of Mr. Frank Kidson, November
29, 1913.)

179–? The Banquet of Thalia. On p. 78 as "The Anacreontic Song." (Text only.
Communication of Mr. Frank Kidson, November 29, 1913, who says that the
song is no longer in the 1812 ed.)

[1796] The Busy Bee, Vol. II. Headed "LXX. Sung by Mr. Bannister at the
Anacreontic. Written by Mr. Thomlinson." (Text only. Communication of Mr. Frank Kidson, November 29, 1913.)

1797. Stewart's Vocal Magazine, Edinburgh, Vol. I. Headed "Song LXXXVII.
To Anacreon in Heaven." (Text and air with bass.)

1799. The London Musical Museum, Glasgow, 1799. On p. 43 as "The Sons of
Anacreon." (Text only. Communication of Mr. Frank Kidson, December 21, 1913.)

1804. The Soul of Harmony, Norwich, plate dated 1804. On p. 1 of pt. II as
"The Anacreontic Song by Ralph Tomlinson, esq." (Text only. Communication of Mr. Frank Kidson, November 29, 1913.)

Smollet Holden, of Dublin, made a curious use of the air by including a "Masonic ode, song and chorus, written by Mr. Connel, on behalf of the Masonic Orphan School," to the air of "To Anacreon in
Heaven" in his "A selection of Masonic Songs." The collection is
undated, but according to Mr. Grattan Flood (under date of January
24, 1910), Holden's book contains a tune with words "by the *late*
celebrated Bro: Robert Burns," so that the date of his death—July
27, 1796—would approximately fix the date of publication of the first
edition. A second edition bears the imprint "Dublin, A. L. 5802"
(A. D. 1802), and Mr. Elson inserted a photographic facsimile of this
Masonic ode, another parody of "To Anacreon in Heaven," (first
words: "To old Hiram, in Heav'n where he sat in full glee") from his
copy of the second edition in his book on the National Music of
America.

This excursion into the history of the Anacreontic Society and into
the bibliographical history of its constitutional song "To Anacreon in
Heaven" has proved at least one important fact:

In view of the contemporary evidence already accumulated, RALPH
TOMLINSON'S AUTHORSHIP OF THE TEXT OF "TO ANACREON IN
HEAVEN" IS CLEAR BEYOND REASONABLE DOUBT and Mr. Grattan
Flood's statement in 1912 that the words "are of Irish origin, and
evidently emanated from Ireland about the year 1765" painfully
betrays its nature of a raw assertion. Irish in origin the text was
only, if Ralph Tomlinson was an Irishman. Mr. Grattan Flood was
prompted to his assertion by an argument hesitatingly advanced by
Mr. Blake, but before long it will be seen how the premise of Mr.
Blake's argument, and therewith the argument itself, collapses.

If it is clear on the one hand that Ralph Tomlinson indeed wrote "To Anacreon in Heaven," it is not clear just when this poem was written by him whom the London Magazine in March, 1780, called the "Late Ralph Tomlinson," thereby establishing (compare also the account in the Gentleman's Magazine) his date of death at the latest as early in 1780.[a]

If Tomlinson was a founder of the Anacreontic Society of London or one of its earliest members, then he might have written his "To Anacreon in Heaven" poem "about 1766," or shortly after this approximate date of foundation of the society given in the Gentleman's Magazine. I am inclined to doubt such an early origin of the poem. Though his poetry is not of a high order, Tomlinson "intwined the myrtle of Venus with Bacchus's vine" with very much more fetching inspiration and spirit than many other poets of fugitive convivial poems of typically eighteenth century Anacreontic atmosphere which I have read. For this reason the poem, even though perhaps at first jealously guarded by the Anacreontic Society against publicity, could not fail to gradually attract attention, and if written "about 1766" its first *definitely* known appearance in fashionable songsters of the time at so late a date as 1778 would be surprising. In fact, it is not unreasonable to surmise that either the writing of the poem led to Tomlinson's election as their president by the enthusiastic "sons of harmony," or that his election as president inspired Tomlinson to write a club song for the Anacreontic Society. Barring indisputable proof of earlier appearance in print, with or without music, this would suggest the years between 1770 and 1776, inclusive of a wide safety margin.

That the text of "To Anacreon in Heaven" existed at the latest in July, 1778, is obvious from its inclusion in the August, 1778, number of the Vocal Magazine.   Mr. Blake's logic that therefore "it is reasonable to suppose that it existed as sheet music at least *two* years before" I am utterly unable to comprehend. Ordinarily the writing and printing of a poem precede its musical setting by a composer, unless the poem is fitted to an existing melody.   If Tomlinson did not utilize an existing melody, then it would be more reasonable to suppose that the text of the poem existed at least two years before it existed as sheet music.   That the song—other considerations aside—"may have

---

[a] The British Museum possesses under Ralph Tomlinson "A slang pastoral; being a parody on a celebrated poem of Dr. Byron's [!].   Written by R. Tomlinson.   London, 1780."

I have been unable to find in the Gentleman's Magazine and several other magazines or in works like Brydges' Censura Literaria, Nichol's Literary Anecdotes, etc., anything further on the career of Ralph Tomlinson; I am therefore not in a position to prove the obvious conjecture that the author of the British Museum pamphlet is identical with the author of "To Anacreon in Heaven."

existed in manuscript many years" before it appeared in print, with or without music, will not be disputed by any author or composer who has had dealings with publishers.

"To Anacreon in Heaven" was written by Ralph Tomlinson, and was adopted as the constitutional song by the Anacreontic Society, founded "about 1766." It could not very well be adopted as such without appropriate music. Hence, unless Tomlinson adapted his poem to an existing melody, the argument will hold good that the music was composed shortly after the completion of the poem, and presumably by a musician who was a member of the society. Both poem and music, of course, must have existed in manuscript before "To Anacreon in Heaven" appeared in print, with or without music. Whether or not the Anacreontic Society jealously guarded its club song against publicity—the best way of accomplishing this was by keeping the song unpublished, but without publication the song could not be copyrighted, a dilemma in which other societies with club songs have found themselves—we do not know, but obviously the text of the song must have been known to the compiler of the Vocal Magazine. Whatever attention "To Anacreon in Heaven" had gained outside of the Anacreontic Society, the poem clearly appealed to the compiler sufficiently for inclusion in the first volume of his collection of—

> The Vocal Magazine . . . containing all the English, Scotch, and Irish Songs . . .
> Glees . . . Ballads, etc., deemed any way worthy of being transmitted to posterity.

Now this collection contains about 1,300 poems (without music). The compilation, selection, distribution, etc., alone of such a vast number of more or less fugitive poems must have kept the compiler busy for many months. Under the circumstances it is just a trifle too fanciful to accuse him, as did Mr. Blake, of deliberately and flagrantly having paraphrased the text of "To Anacreon in Heaven," in order to change the neutral *locale* of the text to London. What earthly object could the compiler have had in picking out exactly "To Anacreon in Heaven" for a flagrant piece of paraphrasing? A diabolical, Machiavellian creature he must have been to include in his collection so many Irish poems and yet to change the phraseology of "To Anacreon in Heaven" so as to fraudulently create in the minds of future historians, bent on investigating the origin of "The Star-Spangled Banner," the impression that this particular poem was of English and not of Irish provenience!

Is is not much more impartial to take it for granted that the compiler of the Vocal Magazine published the poem as it actually read when acquired by him for incorporation in his songster? And, if two different versions of the text existed about the time that he was preparing his accumulation of many hundreds of poems for publication, is it not fair to assume that he knew of only one? Furthermore, if the difference in date between these two versions was but relatively slight, perhaps a difference of only one, two, or three years, is not the surmise reasonable that these textual differences were introduced after the compiler of the Vocal Magazine had acquired the "To Anacreon in Heaven" text for his purposes and that the changes had not yet attracted his attention when he published the text in August, 1778? Indeed, in case that a plausible reason be adduced why the Anacreontic Society should have found it necessary to amend the text of its constitutional song during those years, does it not stand to reason that the compiler of the Vocal Magazine had the earlier, the original, text in his possession for future use and not yet the amended text?

Whether the reader be willing or not to answer these questions in the affirmative, one fact stands out like a rock: The *earliest* known DATED appearance of the text of "To Anacreon in Heaven" is in the Vocal Magazine of 1778. Until a *dated earlier* publication of the text (with or without music) be found or unless circumstantial evidence absolutely forces us to date an *undated* publication *earlier* than 1778, the text of "To Anacreon in Heaven," as it stands in the Vocal Magazine, must be considered for methodological reasons as the *earliest version* of the text extant!

We have seen that the growth of the Anacreontic Society forced it to change quarters repeatedly, until it moved from the London Coffee House on Ludgate Hill to the more spacious Crown and Anchor Tavern in the Strand. By deduction I have suggested 1776 as the year of this removal. Well, then! If the original text of "To Anacreon in Heaven" contained any reference whatsoever to Ludgate Hill, not only can Tomlinson not have written his poem before the (to us unknown) date of the club's removal TO Ludgate Hill, but an amendment of the text became immediately necessary upon the club's removal FROM Ludgate Hill to the Crown and Anchor in the Strand.

Casual comparison of the texts submitted or recorded would reveal no differences except differences of interpunctuation, orthography, and others here negligible. More careful comparison discloses textual differences that shed further light on the bibliographical history of the music of the song, and therewith, as bibliographical research so often does, help to clear out the weeds that have interfered with the normal growth of our knowledge of the song's history.

In the second stanza of the *earliest* known publication and version of the text, in the Vocal Magazine, 1778, the seventh line reads:

A fig for Parnassus: To Rowley's we'll fly

and in the third stanza the second line:

To the hill of old Lud will incontinent flee.

"The hill of old Lud," of course, means old Ludgate Hill, and with this line we find ourselves in the midst of London. "To Rowley's we'll fly" can mean nothing from the context of Tomlinson's poem except that "the yellow-hair'd god and his nine fusty maids" will fly "To Rowley's" to the Anacreontic Society. Apparently we have here an allusion to an inn on Ludgate Hill. "To Rowley's" would either mean in general a "name . . . known to have been common as applied to taverns, in honour of the socalled 'merry monarch,' Charles II," as *X*. in the Musical Times article of 1896 has it, or Rowley's was an inn on Ludgate Hill well known by the name of its proprietor, or an inn well enough known by the proprietor's name to have fitted into the verse with less difficulty and more poetry than the trade name of the inn and without obscurity in the mind of the reader of the poem. In other words, "To Rowley's" suggested to the members the place at which the Anacreontic Society met at the time that the poem was written. Supposing, for instance, that one Rowley was the proprietor of the London Coffee House on Ludgate Hill, even a very minor poet would have had compunctions about writing "To the London Coffee House we'll fly," whereas "To Rowley's we'll fly" was abundantly clear to the initiated and sounded less prosaic.[a]

When the Anacreontic Society, probably in 1776, moved from the London Coffee House on Ludgate Hill to the Crown and Anchor in the Strand, immediately the allusion to the former *locale* of the society was out of place and had to be removed from the text of

---

[a] I have at last, I think, been able to definitely connect the name Rowley with the London Coffee House. In the London Directory for 1799, I find "Rowley and Leech, Wine Merchants, 24 Ludgate Hill" and in John Timbs' book on Clubs and Club life in London (London, 1908), under "London Coffee House": "At the bar of the London Coffee House was sold Rowley's British Cephalic Snuff." This last bit of information is also in Thornbury's "Old and New London," who moreover states (Vol. I, p. 227–228) that the London Coffee House, 24 to 26 Ludgate Hill, was first opened in May, 1731. That Wheatley in "London Past and Present" (Vol. II, p. 426) has the date of opening as late as January 5, 1771, does not conflict with the main point, since from a rough sketch made for me by Miss Constance White (London) of a portion of sheet D2 in R. Horwood's "Plan of the Cities of London and Westminster, 1799 (at the British Museum, also in the Library of Congress), it appears that the London Coffee House occupied the premises on No. 24, *i. e.*, where *Rowley* and Leech held forth as wine merchants. It is quite suggestive, by the way, that, as Miss White found out, in the London directories a James Rowley, Linen draper, of Ludgate St. appears for the first time in 1763, and that he lived from 1768–73 at 29 Ludgate St. Finally, it is also suggestive that the London City directory of 1912 shews at 42 Ludgate Hill "Ye Old London Coffee House," next door to St. Martin Ludgate Church. There it stood in the eighteenth century, too, but the number was then 24 not 42. In 1867 the original house seems to have been closed. According to Wheatley, "The London Coffee House was at one time a great resort of Americans." Stationers' Hall was just around the corner of Rowley's.

this constitutional song.   What was more natural or prudent in view of this experience than to not only amend the text but to so amend it that "To Rowley's we'll fly" and "To the hill of old Lud" were replaced by words of absolutely neutral character without any personal or topographical allusions that might be subject to change at any time?   Now, then, it is a fact that *all texts submitted or recorded above with the only exception of the earliest one known, that in the Vocal Magazine of 1778, have in the second stanza the amended line*

AWAY TO THE SONS OF ANACREON WE'LL FLY

and in the third stanza the amended line

FROM HELICON'S BANKS WILL INCONTINENT FLEE.

These certainly were lines that could be sung anywhere.[a]

Allowing for the hypothetical possibility that the society moved from Rowley's to its new quarters about simultaneously with the insertion of the original instead of the amended text in the Vocal Magazine, or that the editor was just a little behind the times, nevertheless it follows with probability that the amended text can not be dated much earlier than 1776.   Furthermore, if any existing text refers in its title or elsewhere to the "late" Ralph Tomlinson then that particular text can not have been published before the death of Ralph Tomlinson, who apparently died at the latest early in 1780 or at the latest after the printing of his poem in the Vocal Magazine (about August), 1778, where he is not yet called the "late" Ralph Tomlinson.   If, however, a publication says "the late president," then of course these words do not necessarily mean "the president who lately died," but may mean "lately president."   In the latter case the date of the publication would be circumscribed by the terms of Ralph Tomlinson's presidency.   We know from the Gentleman's Magazine that Mr. Mulso succeeded Tomlinson in the chair in 1776 or 1777, but Tomlinson may have been elected president again after the expiration of Mr. Mulso's term.   Finally, if any text refers in its title or elsewhere to the "Crown and Anchor," then it can not have been published until after the society's removal to this tavern, and it follows with necessity that *even the earliest text with the amended topographically neutral lines must be dated later than the removal of the Anacreontic Society from Rowley's on Ludgate Hill to the Crown and Anchor in the Strand.*   In other words, *1776 or later,* if 1776 was the date of the removal.

These are the criteria on which, individually or jointly and together with other incidental criteria, the chronology of undated publications,

---

[a] I hasten to add that the 1781 and 1784 editions of the Vocal Magazine still have "To Rowley's we'll fly" and "To the hill of old Lud."   This is quite natural, since they were merely reissues (without the preface) of the 1778 edition, *not* revised editions.

with or without music, of "To Anacreon in Heaven" will have to be based. My personal impression from all these facts, circumstances, clews, deductions, etc., is that very likely all undated publications of "To Anacreon in Heaven" with the amended text of the song were of later date than 1778, the date of the Vocal Magazine. This personal impression is particularly strong in case of publishers whose career as publishers lasted longer after 1778 than before.

It is now time to apply these and other criteria to three editions of "To Anacreon in Heaven" in sheet-music form, which on purpose have not been drawn into the argument so far. Their titles read:

1a. The Anacreontic Song as Sung at the Crown and Anchor Tavern in the Strand. The words by Ralph Tomlinson Esqr. late President of that Society. Price 6d. London, Printed by Longman & Broderip, 26 Cheapside. (For facsimile of copy in possession of Mr. Frank Kidson see Appendix, Plate VIII.)

1b. Same title but with imprint: Longman & Broderip No. 26 Cheapside and No. 13, Hay Market (Comp. facsimile in Appendix, Plate IX. By permission of the Boston Public Library.)

(1a and 1b consist of a four page folio music sheet; p. [1] blank, on p. 2 air and bass; p. 3 four-part "Chorus" and stanzas 2–6 of text; p. 4 arrangement of the air for guitar and for German flute. Pages 2–3 in 6/4 time. C major.)

2. The Anacreontic Song. As Sung at the Crown and Anchor Tavern in the Strand, London, with General Admiration. [lower margin] Published by Anne Lee in Dame Street (No. 2)

(1p. folio. 6/4 time. D major. Air and bass. Six stanzas of text. No "chorus" or arrangement for other instruments. Compare facsimile in Appendix, Plate III.)

3. The Anacreontic Song. Sung by Mr. Incledon with great Applause. Dublin. Published by E. Rhames, at her Musical Circulating Library, No. 16, Exchange Street.

(1p. folio. 6/4 time. D major. Air and bass. Six stanzas of text, followed by F major arrangement of the air for guitar. No "chorus." Compare facsimile in Appendix, Plate IV.)

These editions, too, have the amended lines "Away to the sons of Anacreon we'll fly" and "From Helicon's banks will incontinent flee." Furthermore, they are all *undated*. Hence, acceptance of the above criteria would establish roughly the date of publication of all three editions as *probably 1776 or later*, if not *probably 1778 or later*. This even without the further arguments presented below.

One of the most useful books to music bibliographers is Mr. Frank Kidson's British Music Publishers, London [1900]. In this we are told that Benjamin Rhames was succeeded by his widow Elizabeth at 16 Upper Blind Quarry "before 1775." Apparently it was this remark which caused Mr. Blake to surmise that her edition of "To Anacreon in Heaven" may have been published as early as 1775. Mr. Blake overlooked the further remark of Mr. Kidson's that "Gilbert's 'Dublin' tells us . . . that about 1776 Upper Blind Quary, in consequence of its evil repute, had its name altered to Exchange Street." It is this address which appears on Elizabeth Rhames's edition of the song and "since she was succeeded by her son, Francis Rhames, probably near the year 1790–5" we have the rather wide range of from "about 1776" to "1790–5" as the possible date of publication of the Rhames edition. But Mr. Blake overlooked another important clew, or at least he does not seem to have realized its importance.   I mean the reference in the title to Charles Benjamin Incledon, the famous English tenor, who possessed a voice of remarkably wide range.   Incledon died in 1826 and he was born in 1763! This year of birth, of course, makes it absolutely impossible to date the Elizabeth Rhames edition anywhere near 1775.   Indeed, since he was in the English navy from 1779 to 1783, since he made his first appearance as a professional singer in 1784, and since there would have been very little business sense in putting the words "Sung by Mr. Incledon with great applause" on a sheet song, before Incledon had become popular enough for his name to attract the attention of the music-buying public, it follows that the Elizabeth Rhames edition of "To Anacreon in Heaven" probably did not appear until after 1784.   Indeed, the fact that Incledon's name figures in a similar manner on Exshaw's publication of "To Anacreon in Heaven" in his London Magazine, September, 1791, would lead one to suspect that Elizabeth Rhames did not publish the song until about 1791. This impression is strengthened by the fact that, as Mr. W. J. Lawrence informed me in his letter of November 15, 1913, "Incledon made his first appearance in Dublin at the Crow Street Theatre on June 20, 1791, remaining there till August 1st."   But, whether 1791 or 1784 be the approximately earliest date, clearly *the Elizabeth Rhames edition can have absolutely no bearing on the early history of " To Anacreon in Heaven,"* and tentative deductions from this edition as to the Irish origin of the text or its original version collapse eo ipso, and pitifully!

According to Mr. Kidson's historical sketch of the important firm of Longman & Co., "in 1779 [the name of] Lukey is absent from the firm, which now remains as Longman & Broderip and exists till 1798 . . .   Before 1785 Longman & Broderip had taken another branch shop at 13 Haymarket" in addition to their place of business at "26 Cheapside."   How long before 1785 this happened Mr. Kidson does not know, but in his letter of November 3, 1913, he tells me that they "were not there much before 1783."

At any rate, Longman & Broderip's earlier issue of "To Anacreon in Heaven" without "13 Haymarket" in the imprint, was not published before 1779 nor after the opening of the Haymarket branch shop.   Incidentally, therefore, this sheet song does not interfere with the conjecture based on the Vocal Magazine that texts (with or without music) which have the amended lines, a reference to the "Crown and Anchor" and a reference to the "late president" Tomlinson, probably appeared later than the Vocal Magazine of 1778. On the contrary, even the earliest Longman & Broderip edition of "To Anacreon in Heaven" corroborates that conjecture.

Mr. Frank Kidson, the possessor of two copies of this exceedingly scarce original Longman & Broderip issue, generously ceded one as gift to the Library of Congress. If merely the fairly frequent issue with the imprint 26 Cheapside *and* 13 Haymarket were extant, it would not be clear that this was merely the reissue of the original with changed imprint. Furthermore, no entry of "To Anacreon in Heaven" will be found in the firm's "Complete Catalogue" dated 1789 (in the Library of Congress) nor in their catalogues of 1781–82, 1786, 1790, as Mr. Kidson, who possesses these and the one of 1789, informed me on November 24, 1913. This, together with the other fact that they advertised "The Anacreontic Song" in a catalogue on verso of index to Warren's thirtieth Collection of Catches, containing the prize-medal catches of 1791 (in the Library of Congress) could have led to the argument that Longman & Broderip did not publish the song until after 1790. Possibly the reissue actually did not appear until then, perhaps because the original edition had become exhausted, but this much is clear that it can not very well have appeared before the firm opened its branch shop at 13 Haymarket. Consequently, if Mr. W. Barclay Squire in his impressive catalogue of printed music in the British Museum added to this reissue (presumably not known to him to be merely a reissue) the date [1780], this date would seem to be too early by a few years and would seem to apply more correctly, if at all, to the original Longman & Broderip issue without 13 Haymarket in the imprint. However, aside from all such bibliographical considerations, hardly any musician who has read the contemporary accounts of the Anacreontic Society will deny that Longman & Broderip published "To Anacreon in Heaven" in the form actually sung by the society, first by an effective solo voice of wide range, and the refrain repeated in chorus.

As to the Anne Lee, Dublin edition, even Mr. Blake granted that its date of publication swings leisurely between February, 1776, when Anne Lee succeeded her husband in business, and the year 1788, when she was out of business. At any rate Mr. Kidson furnishes proof that she was still publishing under her own name in 1781. In her title Anne Lee says "As sung at the Crown and Anchor Tavern in the Strand, London, with general admiration." A plausible inference would be that at that time "To Anacreon in Heaven," or at least the music, was not yet well known in Dublin; otherwise the reference to London would have been wholly unnecessary. Perhaps Anne Lee imported a manuscript copy of words and music, but is it not much more plausible that she simply copied a printed London edition of the song? In that case, we immediately recall the original Longman & Broderip issue of [1780?] and begin to see the reason why the British Museum dated its copy of Anne Lee's edition also as [1780?].

Mr. Kidson says in his letter of November 3, 1913:

> It is without doubt a copy from the Longman sheet, the music however being transposed one note higher & neither Chorus or guitar & flute parts are reprinted.

Comparison proved that the texts are absolutely the same except that, for instance, in the first stanza the Longman edition has "Patron wou'd be," whereas Anne Lee has "Patron would be." As to the music, comparison will show that the Anne Lee edition has not the trill in the last bar, that the chorus refrain is indicated by a dotted line and a repetition sign, that at the word "fiddle" Anne Lee retains the same note as at "voice," instead of as in the Longman edition taking the higher octave, and that at the words "lend you my" faulty printing gives us (at least in the photograph) three natural Bs, instead of D, C sharp, B natural.

Aside from these insignificant differences, the transposed Anne Lee edition shows all the peculiarities in notation, phrasing, harmonization, rhythm, etc., of the Longman & Broderip edition. The probability is therefore pronounced that she indeed used a copy of the Longman & Broderip for her purposes—unless an edition of "To Anacreon in Heaven" turns up of unquestionably earlier date than the Longman & Broderip edition and with which in appearance the Anne Lee edition is even more closely related. Until then, the Anne Lee edition will best be dated as *about 1780 or later*.

A point has been reached to which the last pages have been leading up gradually but systematically.

Said Mr. Grattan Flood in his "Note" of 1908 (1909):

> The words and music of "To Anacreon" were published by Longman & Broderip in 1779–1780, and were reprinted by Anne Lee of Dublin (? 1780) in 1781. Dr. Cummings says that he saw a copy printed by Henry Fought—at least it is made up with single sheet songs printed by Fought—but this is scarcely likely, as Fought did not print after 1770, and the Song and music were not in existence till 1770–71. . ."

Whether or not Mr. Grattan Flood was present at Mr. Cummings's Music Loan Exhibition lecture in 1904 I do not know, nor where, when, and how he got the above information or impression. In his lecture—and it does not detract in the slightest from my respect for Mr. Cummings's scholarly attainments if I say that his casual remarks

about "To Anacreon in Heaven" are not up to his customary standard of carefulness and accuracy—Mr. Cummings simply said: "I have
brought a copy of the original publication of the ode." Nor have I
seen elsewhere any printed statement by Mr. Cummings that "he
saw a copy printed by Fought" (according to Mr. Kidson, November
8, 1913, the correct spelling is Fougt). In reply to a pertinent
inquiry Mr. Cummings sent, under date of November 7, 1908, this
brief note:

> I had a copy of Smith's "To Anacreon" pub.[lished] in 1771. I showed it at
> a public lecture, but cannot now find it. I have two copies of a little later date.
> The first named was a single sheet song.

Mr. Cummings evidently was not willing to commit his memory
under the circumstances on the point of imprint, nor does he make
it clear whether or no Smith's name appeared on the sheet song as
that of the composer. On the other hand, his words would lead us
to believe that the sheet song was actually "pub. in 1771," though
Mr. Cummings by no means says that the sheet song actually contains
this date.

Mr. Cummings added to the casual remarks in his lecture the air
of "To Anacreon in Heaven," and it is suggestive that he gave the
air in C major. Mr. Cummings is not of the kind to simplify music
for babes in the wood. I suspect that the air actually occurred on
that mysterious sheet in C major, the same key in which Longman
& Broderip published their edition. It is to be hoped that Mr. Cummings's sheet song turns up again, so that it may be put under the
bibliographical microscope. If then the criteria enumerated above
be applied, presumably all mystery will disappear and we shall know
just how this particular edition affects the history of "To Anacreon
in Heaven." For reasons unknown to me I received no reply to a
letter addressed by me on the subject to Mr. Cummings under date
of October 30, 1913. However, this much we know from a communication of Mr. James Warrington, the hymnologist, to Father
Henry, that Mr. Cummings sent him a copy of the title of this mysterious sheet song some years ago and that Ralph Tomlinson's name
appeared on it.

The ground has now been prepared and cleared for consideration
of the main question: Who composed "To Anacreon in Heaven"?

Mr. Blake was the first to deny not merely the probability but also
the possibility that John Stafford Smith composed "To Anacreon
in Heaven." Encouraged by his "explosion" and "annihilation"
of John Stafford Smith, Mr. Grattan Flood in his Ave Maria article
of 1912 advanced the theory that the melody is Irish; that it has all
the characteristics of Furlough O'Carolan's "Bumpers, Squire Jones,"
and is most probably his work.

In lieu of argument I simply submit O'Carolan's melody as it stands in Hime's Favourite Collection of O'Carolan's tunes, Dublin [17—]:

BUMPER SQUIRE JONES

Comment, I trust, is superfluous. If this melody of O'Carolan's is the nearest that Mr. Grattan Flood with his very extensive knowledge of Irish music of every description could come to "The Star Spangled Banner," *scil.* "To Anacreon in Heaven," after all these years of enthusiastic research in behalf of Irish music, we may rest assured, that the air of "To Anacreon in Heaven" will not be found in any Irish music publication or manuscript of an authentic and genuine date prior to the time when Ralph Tomlinson wrote the text. Nor has Mr. Frank Kidson, so he informs me, under date of November 3, 1913, run across any melody in British collections, printed or manuscript, that could by any stretch of imagination be identified with the air of "To Anacreon in Heaven." The word of such an authoritative and industrious collector of British folk and popular airs carries tenfold more weight than the statement that I, too, have failed to find any such air in the fairly numerous eighteenth century British song publications in the Library of Congress. On the other hand, some weight may attach to my statement that I have not found the air mentioned in American publications or manuscripts prior to the latter part of the last decade of the eighteenth century.

That single melodic snatches, phrases, motives, or half motives of "To Anacreon in Heaven" are common enough in musical literature, nobody will deny, just as otherwise totally different poems may have words in common, but in its entirety as melody "To Anacreon in Heaven" appears to have had no prototype.[a] Everything, indeed, tends to imply that Ralph Tomlinson did not use an already existing melody but that the melody of "To Anacreon in Heaven" was composed after and not before he wrote his poem.

The reader may ask: Did, perhaps, the founder of the Anacreontic Society, Jack Smith, "a sly dog at a catch" try his hand at Tomlinson's poem? The reader may even suspect some connection between this Jack Smith and John Stafford Smith, so sly a dog at a catch that he repeatedly was given prize medals of the Catch Club, but with such suggestive speculations I shall not concern myself here. Impossible the identity of the two Smiths would not be, though John Stafford Smith was but a youngster "about 1766" when the Anacreontic Society was founded. However, Smith would not have been the first nor the last youngster, as I can testify from personal experience, to have founded a club at so early an age. If Mr. Grattan Flood maintains that John Stafford Smith could not, in 1771, have composed "To Anacreon in Heaven," because Smith's earliest known composition dates from 1773, I fear that his argument will lead us nowhere. Not only is there absolutely no reason why a trained musician of about 21 years should have been too young to compose "To Anacreon in Heaven"—think of the precocity of innumerable composers, great and not great—but Mr. Grattan Flood will find in Thomas Warren's eleventh Collection of Catches, Canons, and Glees [1772] with the prize-medal pieces of 1772 on pages 10–16, the four-part canzonet "Stay, Shepherd, Stay," and on pages 32–37 the glee "Sleep, Poor Youth," both printed as by John Stafford Smith.

If Smith was a *printed* composer in 1772, it stands to reason that he was not quite a novice in setting music to texts that struck his fancy. But, as I have said, such speculation leads us nowhere, except to demonstrate that John Stafford Smith, if called upon at that time, could have composed Tomlinson's "To Anacreon in Heaven" about 1771. And, if the poem was not written until about 1775, then, of

---

[a] As a pleasant pastime I suggest to the reader to slightly shift the rhythm of the following melody and he will have the beginning of our "Star Spangled Banner."

Air XI. BUSH OF BOON

For the benefit of those who might have no hesitation in asserting that the tune of "To Anacreon in Heaven" shows all the characteristics of "Bush of Boon," and most probably is the same, my source may here be mentioned: Fielding's ballad farce "An Old Man Taught Wisdom," London, J. Watts, 1735, where the tune is sung to the words "Oh, dear papa! don't look so grum."

course, all chronological scruples vanish absolutely, because by that time John Stafford Smith had gained distinction as a composer.

Since the rumor that Dr. Samuel Arnold composed "To Anacreon in Heaven" has been silenced by unanimous consent, and since John Stafford Smith is the only other British composer to whom that honor has been credited with sound argument, I here restrict myself absolutely to the arguments for and against his authorship. It so happened that Rev. H. T. Henry, of Philadelphia, took up the cudgels for John Stafford Smith against Mr. Blake and Mr. Grattan Flood exactly at the time that I was preparing a revised edition of my "Star-Spangled Banner" chapter. In order to preserve as much as possible its nature of a "Report," in order to give Father Henry all credit due him, and because we found ourselves in accord on such vital arguments as are now ripe for presentation, Father Henry's essay in the Records of the American Catholic Historical Society (Dec., 1913) will now be drawn upon to establish, if possible, the composer of "To Anacreon in Heaven."

First of all, it is but fair to look into Mr. Blake's and Mr. Grattan Flood's attacks on John Stafford Smith's veracity and character as a gentleman. Says Father Henry in this connection, on pages 329–333:

> I do not know with what intent Dr. Flood introduces his remark concerning the "audacity" of Smith, in the following paragraph; but I may fairly conjecture that the purpose was to impugn Smith's trustworthiness when, in 1799, he claimed that the air of "Anacreon" was "harmonized by the author." This conjecture is not, indeed, very logical, because Mr. Blake and, following him, Dr. Flood, contend that by "author" Smith did *not* mean "composer." The major part of Mr. Blake's and Dr. Flood's argument turns on *this* (to their minds *obvious*) interpretation of "author;" and accordingly both should most earnestly affirm the absolute trustworthiness of Smith. That Smith's veracity should be impeached (and, of all men, by the two consentient interpreters of Smith's own words) is not, of course, a logical thing; but I am at a loss how else to interpret Dr. Flood's indignation at Smith's "audacity." But now to his impeachment of Smith:

>> An examination of Smith's *Fifth Book of Cazonets* reveals not only the interesting fact that this fourth-rate musician merely *arranged* the long-existing melody of "Anacreon," but he also arranged in a different volume another Anacreontic song and likewise "God Save the King!" and had the audacity to assert that "the whole was *composed* by John Stafford Smith about the year 1780." (The italics are Dr. Flood's.)

> The hastily-written English of this paragraph might easily mislead the reader. It is not an examination of Smith's Fifth Book which will reveal to us his composition of "another Anacreontic song, and likewise 'God Save the King!' . . . ," etc. These things were revealed to Mr. Blake when he came across the 1780 volume of Smith's in an old bookshop in London.

> But once more to our sheep. Dr. Flood marvels at the audacity of Smith in declaring that he had composed the whole of a volume containing "God Save the King!" Readers who are not familiar with the long controversies waged about the text and tune of the British national anthem will fail to realize fully the enormous audacity of Smith in claiming that air as his own composition . . .

Had Smith . . . declared that he was the composer of an air which so many people could testify that they had heard sung or had seen in print before he was born, his act would not have been one of "audacity," but rather one of the greatest foolhardiness possible to mortal man. With about equal foolishness might the present writer claim to have composed the "Star-Spangled Banner."

Dr. Flood could not but know that the anthem was popular before Smith was born; and it is indeed because of this knowledge that he charges Smith with "audacity." I am not enough of a psychologist to explain how, under these circumstances, Dr. Flood could have considered Smith's act "audacious" rather than idiotic. He must (I presume) have "complacently followed" Mr. Blake down the rushing tide of the latter's mistaken enthusiasm. For Mr. .Blake had discovered Smith's volume published in 1780, in an old bookshop in London; had purchased it for 80 cents (although, as he remarks, he would gladly have given $8, and adds—jocularly, I suppose—that he would sell it to Congress for $800); had found "God Save the King" in it; had read on the title page that Smith composed the "whole" of the volume and had been properly scandalized at such incomprehensible audacity. But Mr. Blake was not a musician; he was an inventor of a device for rifles, and his invention was adopted (so the biographical note affixed to the binding of his pamphlet tells us) by the United States in the Spanish-American War. That Dr. Flood should have "complacently followed" Mr. Blake is the truly wonderful thing; for Dr. Flood is a musician, as well as a historian of music, and should immediately have suspected that something was "out of gear" in Mr. Blake's views concerning Smith's claim to the authorship of the British national anthem. A few moment's inspection of the volume itself would have enlightened him as to the exact claim of Smith, but he followed Mr. Blake, whose offer to sell the book to Congress was quite superfluous, for Congress possesses both the 1780 volume and that of 1799.

What, then, is the explanation of the mystery of Smith's audacity? In his letters to me of 18 and 27 October, Mr. Sonneck tells simply and clearly what it really was that Smith laid claim to as composer:

"Blake refers to the words, 'the whole compos'd by John Stafford Smith,' on "the title-page of his A Miscellaneous Collection of New Songs, Catches, and "Glees, London, James Blundell (published, as the contents prove, in the year "1780), and deduces his imputation that Smith fraudulently claimed with the "above words to have been the composer of 'God Save the King' from the "fact that on p. 27 'God Save the King' appears in 'A Canon in Subdiapente; "2 in 1 on a plain Song.' Mr. Blake, who is not by profession a musician or "historian, breaks down under his own argument by quoting Smith's Index, in "which this particular piece appears as 'Si Deus pro nobis . . . Canon . . . 27.' "The puzzle is simple enough for a musician: 'Si Deus pro nobis' are the "words put to the 'Canon in Subdiapente; 2 in 1,' and the 'plain song,' or "'cantus firmus,' as we would say nowadays, on which Smith composed his "canon was the melody of 'God Save Great George our King,' duly printed "with these words. . . . Dear old Smith's Index shows to what he laid claims "as 'composer' of 'the whole': the canon (as was correct) and nothing "more."[a]

---

[a] On p. 32 of the same collection Smith has "A Canon on a ground bass; real London Cries." According to the logic of Mr. Blake and Mr. Grattan Flood this would mean that Smith, claiming to be the composer of "The whole" collection, had the audacity to pose as the composer of these "real London Cries." I can not make myself believe that John Stafford Smith was quite such an audacious idiot as all that.

Though my quotation of O'Carolan's sprightly air of "Bumper, Squire Jones" makes further comparison of it with "To Anacreon in Heaven" unnecessary, I can not abstain from treating the reader to at least part of Rev. Henry's deliciously humorous and for Mr. Flood really disastrous

COMPARISON OF "BUMPER" WITH "ANACREON."

As already stated, the only argument of apparent value advanced by Dr. Flood for the Irish origin of the air of our national anthem is the one he bases on musical "characteristics," for the melody of "Anacreon" has, he declares, "all the characteristics" of O'Carolan's "Bumper, Squire Jones." He invites his readers to make the comparison, assuring them that the truth of his assertion "can easily be tested" in this way. The test is not, however, quite so easily made, for the readers must catch their hare first—must first of all find O'Carolan's air—and then must proceed to cook it, as it were, in the same pot with "Anacreon."

To facilitate for them the process of comparison, I have transposed "Anacreon" from the key of C into the "Bumper" [condensation used by Rev. Henry merely in the interest of brevity] key of B-flat, and have turned its 6-4 time into the 6-8 time of "Bumper." Something is lost to my demonstration of the dissimilarity between the two airs by this change in the apparent rhythm of "Anacreon"— this change of quarter notes into eighth notes; for the tendency is a natural (although not, it is true, a necessary) one, to sing 6-8 faster than 6-4 time, and to give "Anacreon" something of the rollicking gait of "Bumper." We are thus tempted to turn what may have been a fairly slow or at least a fairly moderate *tempo* of "Anacreon" into what was most probably a fairly fast *tempo* of "Bumper." But if the comparison is to be made with ease and some approximation to accuracy, the change of "Anacreon" to the same key and the same apparent rhythm as those of "Bumper" is almost a necessity. . . .

. . . The only characteristic in which "Bumper" and "Anacreon" agree is the apparently perfect agreement to disagree perfectly; for where one melody ascends the other descends, and vice versa. This agreement to disagree begins with the very first notes and continues throughout to the end, except in the first half of the eleventh bar. So true is this that if the reader looks at any two connected staves, he will fancy that he is gazing at an illustration of scholastic counterpoint in contrary motion. If he should have a very literal mind, he will gravely count the notes on which the two melodies agree as they pass each other, and will not be surprised that they are so very few in number. The "Anacreon" air has 100 notes, and only 7 of these coincide with notes in O'Carolan's air. Seven per cent is not a notable agreement.

. . . The comparison of the tunes of "Bumper" and "Anacreon" makes the contention of Dr. Flood unacceptable to us. If "Bumper" is characteristically Irish, then its antithesis, "Anacreon," must be characteristically non-Irish. But the matter is even more curious than this. After I had transcribed the "Bumper" song from an antique volume of music, I chanced to look over the chapter on disputed ascriptions in O'Neill's Irish Folk Music, and there learned that— mirabile dictu—the tune of "Bumper" had been adjudged *English* by Burk Thumoth (who in 1720 published the first collections of Irish airs), who placed it among the "Twelve English Airs" in his second volume. Hereupon O'Neill remarks that the air is duly accredited to O'Carolan in The Hibernian Muse, "the editor of which in this instance ventured to doubt Thumoth's infallibility." Can humor further go?

COMPARISON OF CHARACTERISTICS

On pages 312–323 Rev. Henry deals with "the negative argument" as follows:

I think the question of the authorship of the tune has been simplified by elimination of the Irish claim (so far, of course, as that claim rests on the bases furnished by Dr. Flood's article). We are now able to consider the effect of Mr. Blake's discovery on the commonly accepted view that Smith is the author. In rejecting this view (which had in 1909 been held by him) Dr. Flood writes:

In order to bolster up Stafford Smith's claim as a composer of the tune, Chappell and his copyists give the date of his Fifth Book of Canzonets as "1780 or 1785." Fortunately for historical accuracy, a wealthy Irish-American, Mr. John Henry Blake, went to the copyright office, Stationers' Hall, London, and searched the record indexes of the copyright department from 1746 to 1799, inclusively, with the result that he discovered the actual date on which Smith entered the copyright, namely, May 14, 1799. [*recte* May 8. Sonneck.]

Dr. Flood is very severe on "Chappell and his copyists," who attempted to "bolster up" Smith's claim by assigning too early a date for his volume. But as late as 1909 Dr. Flood himself wrote in Church Music:

The most decisive proof of the fact that the tune was composed by Smith is the fact that he includes it in his Fifth Collection of Canzonets, Catches, etc., in 1781.

Shall we reckon Dr. Flood among the "copyists" who attempted to "bolster up" Smith's claim by assigning a date for his volume at least 18 years before the appearance of the volume?

. . . This "Fifth Book of Canzonets," then, is the book whose date of copyright was found (in October, 1910) by Mr. John Henry Blake, an American, after a search in the records of Stationers' Hall, London, from the dates 1746–1799. He located the copyright entry of the Fifth Book of Canzonets as 8 May, 1799, and notes a misprint of the title (as given above by Mr. Sonneck) of which he furnishes a photographic facsimile in his monograph. The period-mark placed before "The Anacreontic, and other popular songs," should be a comma, and the word "The" should begin with a small letter—thus associating, Mr. Blake argues, the Anacreontic, not with "other popular songs," but with the previously mentioned "glees." Mr. Blake elevates into a point of capital importance what is merely a printer's error.

. . . Mr. Blake's very argument may be neatly turned against himself. Mr. Sonneck, in letters to me dated October 18 and 27, 1913, does this in the following manner:

"Mr. Blake is correct in stating that in my transcript of the title of Smith's "Fifth Book there is an error. It should be 'author of the favorite glees . . . "Hark the hollow woods, etc. the Anacreontic, and other popular songs,' and "not 'woods, etc. The Anacreontic . . .' (the printer did not follow copy, "but followed office rules in using a capital letter after a period sign, and when "reading proof under pressure of other business I overlooked the error). "Mr. Blake waxes enthusiastic over this discovery, claiming that Smith by "using the lower case letter in 'the' included 'the Anacreontic' among his "aforesaid *glees* composed by him and not among his 'popular songs.' There- "fore, as 'To Anacreon in Heaven' first appeared as a song, not as a glee, Smith "himself did not claim to have composed it, etc. All nonsense, of course, but "it is this kind of nonsense which one has to combat. The very fact, it seems "to me, that the title reads 'etc. the' shows that 'the Anacreontic' belongs "grammatically to 'and other popular songs' and that 'the Anacreontic' was "meant as a 'song'; and the word 'other,' it further seems to me, compels "this interpretation. And again Mr. Blake breaks down under his own infor- "mation, because, as if the registrar wished to make the point raised by me

"above perfectly clear, he transcribed Smith's copyright certificate for Mr.
"Blake as follows: 'the Hollow Woods, etc., The Anacreontic, and other
"popular songs.' "[a]

. . . Continuing the narrative of Blake's discoveries, Dr. Flood writes in the
Ave Maria:

> He also found indisputable evidence that Smith merely *arranged* the tune in the form of a "glee,"
> and that he did not claim any copyright for the tune.

The "indisputable evidence" seems to have been the fact that Smith, in his
Fifth Book of Canzonets (copyrighted May 8, 1799), writes that the tune was
"harmonized by the author." What does "author" mean here? Does it mean
the author (that is, the compiler and editor) of the Fifth Book, namely, Smith;
or does it mean the author (that is, the composer) of the tune? Blake contends
that "author" can not mean "composer" . . .

A reader who is not well versed in the literature of the present discussion
might perhaps suppose that Mr. Blake had "discovered" in Smith's Fifth Book
the phrase "harmonized by the author" in reference to the song "To Anacreon in
Heaven." Not only was the phrase and its relation to the song well known long
since, but a facsimile of the page (in the Fifth Book) containing that phrase
appeared in Mr. Sonneck's Report in 1909.

Again, Smith does not refer to his arrangement of "Anacreon" as a "glee."
It is not wrong so to characterize his composition; but he himself did not so
characterize it. He called it "Anacreontick Song."

As will be seen further on, the copyright certificate appears to establish the
meaning of "author" to be nothing less than "composer." He was the author
(composer) of the "whole" work, the tune of the Anacreontic Song included.

Where, then, is the "indisputable evidence" that Smith "merely *arranged* the
tune in the form of a 'glee'"?

The remaining argument against Smith's authorship of the tune is stated by
Dr. Flood in the Ave Maria as follows:

> Smith lived till the year 1836, and he never asserted his claim as composer of his melody, although
> Key had written "The Star-Spangled Banner" to it in 1814. Surely it stands to reason that if Smith
> had composed the tune, and that the said tune (whether set to "Anacreon in Heaven" and the "Star-
> Spangled Banner") had been sung, printed, and circulated all over the British possessions and in
> America, he would, as a true Britisher, have asserted his claim to it.

Here much is made of Smith's failure to lay claim to the authorship of the tune.
In his Fifth Book of Canzonets, etc., Smith did declare that the tune there given
was "harmonized by the Author." Blake (and, following his lead, Flood) can
see in this declaration only a confession that Smith was not the author of the
tune, but merely the author of the collection; and that if Smith desired to vin-
dicate his authorship of the tune, he should have used the word "composer"
instead of "author." Mr. Kidson could not see the force of this contention. In
his Report Mr. Sonneck had already discussed (p. 23) this interesting question:

> The words "harmonized by the author" may of course mean harmonized by the author of the
> collection and do not necessarily mean harmonized by the author of the air, but these words, together
> with the fact that the collection contains none but Smith's own glees, etc., and the wording of the
> title renders it probable that Smith refers to himself as the composer of the music. . . . Probably
> Smith composed it, if he really did compose the tune, as a song for one voice, and in "harmonizing"
> it for several and different voices he felt obliged to wander away from the original.

---

[a] The transcript of the record made in November, 1913, for the Library of Congress
reads, "Woods, etc., the Anacreontic, and." In other words, if this "t" instead of
a "T" in "the" is correct, then the registrar followed Smith's title exactly, adding
the comma between etc. and the in order to make matters absolutely clear.

This brief extract from the Report shows us that Mr. Sonneck (a) held his judgment in suspense as to the meaning of "author," and (b) had not committed himself—("if he really did compose the tune" are his words)—to the common ascription of the air to Smith. But here it is highly interesting to note with what felicity he is able to make use of the copyright certificate subsequently given to Mr. Blake by the registrar of Stationers' Hall records, to emphasize (almost, if not indeed quite, to the point of conviction) the contention that Smith really did mean by the word "author" nothing less than "composer." This interesting argument is thus stated in Mr. Sonneck's letters to me (18 and 27 October, 1913):

"Now the copyright record, as quoted with great glee but little understanding "by Mr. Blake, distinctly says under 'Property of:' 'Author,' and under "'Share:' 'Whole.' Consequently, if copyright certificates have any evidential "value at all, Smith was officially recorded as claiming the copyright in the "whole 'Fifth Book' as 'Author' (i. e., composer, because to my knowledge "*author* was the official term used in the statute for all copyrightable matter, in- "cluding musical works, and not *composer a* and author can mean in this instance "and under the circumstances composer only and nothing else, since Smith does "not pose as *compiler* of the music, much less as *author* of the texts (in several "instances he mentions the authors of the texts). *Ergo*, if his words on p. 33: "'The Anacreontick *Song* (sic! poor Mr. Blake) harmonized by the author' could "leave the doubt expressed on p. 23 of my 'Report' as to what Smith meant "by these words, these words in conjunction with Smith's copyright certificate "now would appear to establish, beyond reasonable doubt, that Smith *claimed* "to be the author (composer) of '*The* Anacreontick *Song*': 'To Anacreon in "Heaven,' 'harmonized' by him in this 'Fifth Book' as a part-song, and "designated a *glee* by me in my 'Report' (but not by Smith himself!).

"And this (it seems to me) inevitable conclusion stops up the keyhole, which "Mr. Blake can not keep open for escape, that there is in Smith's Miscellaneous "Collection of 1780, on p. 35, a four-part piece headed simply 'Anacreontic.' "In the index it is called, 'Is it summer . . . GLEE.' Thereby Mr. Blake, "or anybody else, is enjoined from operating with the over-nice distinction be- "tween 'song' and 'glee' (*i. e.*, only when it suits their purpose). They can "not say that Smith, in the title-page of his 'Fifth Book,' referred to this 'glee' "as *the popular* Anacreontic *song* composed by him and not to 'Anacreon in "Heaven.' No, the title-page apparently refers to 'Anacreon in Heaven,' and to "this *Anacreontick Song* (popularly known as *the* Anacreontick song) in a *harmon-* "*ized* version Smith laid copyright claim on "May 8, 1799, as author (composer).

---

a Mr. Ernest Bruncken, Assistant Register of Copyright in the Library of Congress, had the kindness to inform me as follows:

Musical copyright. The first case is that of Bach *v.* Longman (Cowp., 623), in 1777. Held, that the same rules apply to both literary and musical compositions, because the words of the act of 1710, "books or other writings," were not confined to letters and language only.

In D'Almaine *v.* Boosey (1 Y. & C. Exch., 299) it is stated as a fact that "a great deal of music" was entered at Stationers' Hall as books; and as a matter of law that "printed music, in whatever form it may be published, is to be considered in refer- ence to copyright proceedings as books."

The terms "author" and "composer" seem to be in use interchangeably. In the statute the word "author" only is used.

"Musical composition" as a special object of protection by copyright is not men- tioned in these terms in any copyright acts of Parliament until the act of 1842.

" Perhaps he lied; but it is up to our friends Blake and Grattan Flood to prove
"that he lied.   Until they produce proof of fraudulent claim, Smith's *claim* at
"least will stand good in any court of scientific inquiry, and I can not see how,
"under the circumstances, we can deny that Smith composed 'To Anacreon in
"Heaven,' unless a prior authenticated claim by some other composer is pro-
"duced.

"And with [*read* in view of] Smith's own copyright claim the silly argument
"collapses that, if Smith had been the composer, he would have taken pains to
"tell the world that he was the composer.   Well, he did, on May 8, 1799, and
"that is all there is to this phase of the matter at present, so far as I can see."

To sum up: Even the most obstinate opponent of Smith has so far
not denied that, "To Anacreon in Heaven" excepted, John Stafford
Smith was the *composer* of the music in his Fifth Book.   The word
author used by Smith in the title, in the copyright entry, and in the
dedication to Viscount Dudley and Ward, where he says: "These glees
and songs . . . are . . . humbly inscribed by the obliged author,"
has so far not been denied to be the equivalent not merely of *compiler* of the collection called Fifth Book, but of *composer* of the music
therein contained, with exception of the disputed "To Anacreon in
Heaven."   Should now the opponents of John Stafford Smith deny
that he was the actual composer of all other music contained in the
Fifth Book, in order to operate with the word "author" in the sense
of "compiler" with special reference to "To Anacreon in Heaven,"
then the burden of proof would be entirely on their shoulders.   Their
mere denial will be valueless in a court of scientific inquiry until such
proof is furnished.   Until then the word "author" used by Smith,
as occasionally by other eighteenth century composers, will be con-
strued by every unbiased historian in its, under the circumstances,
most natural and indeed obvious sense of *composer*.

"To Anacreon in Heaven" became popularly known, as the reader
can not fail to have noticed, as " *The* Anacreontick Song."   Of the
many Anacreontic songs of the time it appears to have been the only
one to have gained such distinction.   In the title of his Fifth Book
John Stafford Smith calls himself the author of "the Anacreontic,
and other popular songs."   In the copyright entry of this Fifth Book
on May 8, 1799, Smith laid copyright claim to the whole book as
author.   On page 33 of this Fifth Book "To Anacreon in Heaven"
appears in a version "harmonized by the author."   Though, if so
inclined, one may designate this arrangement as a glee, Smith himself did not so designate it.   He headed this harmonized version of
"To Anacreon in Heaven" simply as "The Anacreontick Song," and
in the index "To Anacreon in Heaven . . . harmonized" is one of
the only two pieces in the book called "Song."   If an obstinate
opponent of Smith's claim argues that, strictly speaking, "harmonized by the author" may mean harmonized by the author of the
words, Ralph Tomlinson, then the deduction is all the more inevitable

that John Stafford Smith claimed to be the author of the music (i. e. *composer*) of "The Anacreontick Song" with "To Anacreon in Heaven" as text.

Without unduly wishing to influence readers of this revised "Report" one way or the other, self-protection against misrepresentation demands that I put myself squarely on record with this personal opinion:

> Available evidence, and a more thorough study of it, than in 1909, together with the deductive force of Mr. Blake's discovery of the copyright entry of Smith's Fifth Book compel me to believe that the music of RALPH TOMLINSON'S POEM "TO ANACREON IN HEAVEN" WAS INDEED COMPOSED BY JOHN STAFFORD SMITH. Words and music of this song, later on popularly known as "The Anacreontick Song," probably originated about the year 1775; at any rate, before the Anacreontic Society moved from Ludgate Hill, London, to the Crown and Anchor Tavern in the Strand.[a]

One may indeed express surprise that John Stafford Smith waited until 1799 before he publicly claimed the music of "To Anacreon in Heaven" as his own. But are we really certain that he did not claim it years before? May there not be hidden away somewhere in "the wreck of time"—Bacon's beautiful phrase used by Rev. Henry— direct evidence of Smith's authorship, if not his own manuscript, then perhaps some reference in contemporary letters or the like? Even in the absence of such evidence, so late a claim as that of Smith would not be without a parallel. Rev. Henry strikingly illustrates this by pointing to Father Clarence Walworth's translation "Holy God, we praise thy name" of the "Te Deum," published anonymously in 1853 in a Redemptorist "Mission Book." His hymn found its way into many books, Catholic and Protestant, but this translation was never printed with his name until 1880 and then in an "Evangelical Hymnal." Father Walworth himself did not publicly lay claim to his hymn until 1888, when he published his "Andiatoroctè, etc.,"

---

[a] On purpose the method of fixing authorship by "internal evidence," "stilistic characteristics," etc., was not dragged into this matter. Legitimate enough and necessary where no binding proof of authorship in the hand of the author or no positive claim by him of authorship exists, it is often an unsafe method and lends itself easily to pedantry or preconceived preferences. It is doubly unsafe in our case. Neither do the few bars of "To Anacreon in Heaven" abound in stilistic peculiarities, nor do the five books of Smith's music reveal stilistic characteristics sufficiently tangible for profitable comparison with "To Anacreon in Heaven." My impression is that the music in these five books, on the whole, does not conjure memories of "To Anacreon in Heaven," though now and then, as in Smith's prize medal glee of 1777 "Return blest days" at the words "Breast if e'er my cheek" (*In* Smith's "Select collection of catches . . .") I was startlingly reminded of "To Anacreon in Heaven." However, such impressions are too personal to be of any evidential value.

that is, 35 years after it had first appeared in print[!] "Supposing," says Rev. Henry, the Evangelical Hymnal of 1880 "had disappeared and Father Walworth had not lived to bring out his volume of poems, we should not find it an easy matter to settle at this late day the question of authorship. *Late day*—but 13 years after his death."

We, who daily have to catalogue music, know best how much anonymous music exists in manuscript and in print. Some composer must be responsible for the individual piece, but it is the exception, rather than the rule, if circumstantial evidence enables us to credit the music with some degree of certainty to its composer. The path of cataloguers and bibliographers would be smooth indeed, though perhaps less interesting, if signposts so prominent as in the case of "To Anacreon in Heaven" always guided them in their work. Very often we have to struggle forward without such signposts. An author or composer is at perfect liberty to withhold his authorship of a work from the public or not. He may have reasons for keeping a work anonymous that influence him more than the considerations of glory or of the convenience of cataloguers, historians, and readers. He runs the risk of never being identified with a work that may live through many centuries as a master work, but we have no right to quarrel with him for running such a risk. If he finally, after many years, and again for reasons, known or unknown to us, does consent to lift the veil of anonymity, at least we bibliographers feel grateful, do not quarrel with him, give him the benefit of the doubt, and do not cast suspicions on his tardy claim of authorship, unless compelled by convincing evidence to the contrary.

Mr. Blake's patient search through the Stationers' Hall records from 1746 to 1799 and search through the same records from 1770 to 1800, undertaken in 1913 for the Library of Congress, have made it fairly certain that "To Anacreon in Heaven" was not entered in any form for copyright either by the composer or by a publisher prior to May 8, 1799.[a] Now, mere copyright entry will never *prove* authorship eo ipso. If a piece of music is entered for copyright, the presumption of authorship will of course be so strongly in favor of the composer mentioned that bibliographers or historians will accept his authorship in the absence of proof to the contrary. However, the moment their suspicions are aroused, they will look upon a copyright entry as, what historically considered it really is, a mere

---

[a] The only time that "To Anacreon in Heaven" was incidentally mentioned in these records from 1770 to 1800 appears to have occurred when P. Jung on February 9, 1793 "entred for his Copy The Knave's Necklace, or Every Rogue a Halter, a new Anacreontic, the words by a gentleman. Sung at a loyal Association at T—r previous to burning Tom Paine in Effigy to the Tune of To Anacreon in Heaven." This is again (indirect) proof that the tune was not protected by copyright and could be used for other than the original words.

piece of circumstantial evidence of authorship, and will insist on other corroborative evidence, at the very least, in the particular publication itself.[a] On the other hand, neglect of copyright entry may invalidate a composer's proprietory rights legally, but never his authorship historically, if such authorship can be proved by direct or indirect evidence.   This is the case of "To Anacreon in Heaven," where Smith's copyright claim *together* with other evidence has established his musical authorship beyond reasonable doubt.

Had Smith or a publisher registered "To Anacreon in Heaven" at Stationers' Hall immediately upon publication, they could have vindicated the copyright of the song as Rev. Henry pointed out "nowhere save in Great Britain:"

> The English copyright law then in existence did not extend to Ireland until after the Act of Union in 1800. . . .   English copyrighted books were freely published in Dublin and sometimes, to the great annoyance of English publishers, were carried into England . . . in the American colonies, the Revolution removed publishers from all liability to English law, whether statute or common and . . . the British colonies were not under the operation of the English copyright law. If Smith . . . as might easily have been the case, had transferred his common-law right to the publisher of some "collection" of music, his name would not appear in the records of Stationers' Hall.

Once copyright entry was neglected, Smith was practically powerless to stop piracy of his song in its original form (piracy in the ethical, not in the legal sense) even in Great Britain.   His only opportunity for a copyright claim after that would have been to register the song in an *arrangement*.   By the copyright act then in force an author could obtain copyright for two terms of 14 years each, or for a possible total of 28 years.   Now, there is a very remote possibility that "To Anacreon in Heaven" was first published in 1771, i. e. exactly 28 years before 1799.   A peculiar coincidence this is, and shrewdly Rev. Henry seizes upon it, for a possible explanation of entry.   Smith waited until 1799 before he laid claim to "To Anacreon in Heaven" because

> Had Smith written his tune in 1770–1771, his right to it could not survive the year 1799; and it is quite permissible to suppose that he was ready, in that year, with an arrangement of the tune as a glee, so that a new term of copyright might be granted him.

---

[a] As an illustration of how valueless a mere copyright entry may become for purely historical purposes, I submit the following case recently brought to my attention. A young and fairly well known composer submitted the manuscript of a song to a prominent American publisher for publication. Had the publisher accepted it, the song in due course of time would have been registered for copyright and this song *in the form published* would probably have been legally safe against reprint not only, but the presumption of authorship would have been very strongly and permanently in favor of the composer mentioned. The firm's "tester" of manuscripts had his suspicions aroused by some melodic phrase in the song and he found that, though the text was new, the music was practically identical with that of one of Schubert's beautiful but fairly unknown songs. Needless to say, this song by Schubert "composed" by the audacious young gentleman was not published, at any rate not by that particular firm.

Of course, the new term of copyright would have applied to "To Anacreon in Heaven" in its "harmonized" version, but not in its original form as song for one voice,[a] which had become public property.

Personally, I doubt very much that "To Anacreon in Heaven" was published as a sheet song as early as 1771. I also doubt that Smith's inclusion of it in a "harmonized" version in his Fifth Book was due to any special consideration of the copyright laws. I am inclined to believe that it simply had struck Smith's fancy as a composer to

---

[a] As stated in my "Report" of 1909, the "Anacreontic Songs for 1, 2, 3 & 4 voices composed and selected by Doctr. Arnold and dedicated by permission to the Anacreontic Society. London. Printed for J. Bland, No. 45 Holborn, 1785" and, so a manuscript note in the Library of Congress copy informs us, "pubd. as the Act directs 4th June 1785" do *not* include "To Anacreon in Heaven." In this very scarce collection Arne, Arnold, Baildon, Boyce, Green, Händel, etc. are mentioned as composers but not John Stafford Smith. Now, there occurs on the pictorial title-page an obvious allusion to Tomlinson's poem, since *Momus with his risible phiz* is pictured showing to *old Thunder* "The humble *petition* of the members of the Anacreontic." In addition some kind of a winged being with a herald's trumpet is bearing a legend "Anacreontic Society." Under these circumstances, we certainly have a right to wonder at the exclusion of the society's by that time fairly famous constitutional song from Arnold's collection. Rev. Henry advances this explanation: "Apparently some copyright law forbade the inclusion of the tune. If, at that early day, nobody *claimed* it, it seems hard to explain, why, of all the songs open to Dr. Arnold for inclusion, it should have been passed over in silence." Difficult of proof, as this explanation is, it is plausible. Of course, the puzzle would disappear if it should turn out that the Library of Congress copy is incomplete and should really contain also "To Anacreon in Heaven." The make-up of the collection is peculiar. After the title page (verso blank) come p. [1], 2–63. On verso of this p. 63 begins Arnold's song "Flow thou regal purple stream" from his "Castle of Andalusia" and the song has the pagination 2–4. With it our copy stops. There is no index and nothing to indicate that our copy is incomplete, but as it appears to coincide with that at the British Museum, it probably is complete. On the other hand there are plenty of indications that previously published music plates had simply been pressed into service for this compilation by Arnold. Supposing, then, that minute bibliographical research should establish the fact that the book, with exception perhaps of one or two compositions by Arnold, contains *none but songs, etc., previously published on plates of the same size*, would not that fact suggest perhaps the probability that Bland did not care to go to the expense of engraving and printing music still in manuscript? If "To Anacreon in Heaven" in 1785 was still in manuscript, i. e. as sung by the "Anacreontic Society," would not that fact, then, furnish another plausible explanation, why the song was not inserted by Arnold? Of course, "To Anacreon in Heaven" can not very well have been in manuscript in 1785 in the form as sung by the "Anacreontic Society," if Longman & Broderip, who published the song with the double address of the firm in the imprint, had actually opened their branch shop at 13, Haymarket before 1785. With just a little imagination, one may stumble upon other explanations. For instance, there may have existed intense professional rivalry between Smith and Arnold, and Smith may have forbidden the insertion of his song in a compilation by Arnold or Arnold did not care to insert music by Smith; or, the Anacreontic Society viewed the publicity its constitutional song had already gained with displeasure and (in vain) did all in its power to prevent further publicity. I leave it to others to indulge in futile speculation along these lines, but, to repeat it, if Arnold had composed "To Anacreon in Heaven" he presumably would have inserted it in the collection.

"harmonize" his song or that somebody, perhaps members of the Anacreontic Society, had suggested an arrangement of his and their "To Anacreon in Heaven" as a glee for club purposes. I am all the more inclined to such a simple explanation, because Smith's other collections did not always contain his music in its orginal form. For instance, in his Miscellaneous Collection of New Songs, [1780] his "Chearful glee" (on p. 42) had been "alter'd & adapted for treble voices" by him.

Those who with Mr. Blake take it for granted that John Stafford Smith was a "good business man" probably will still insist on asking: Does it not stand to reason that Smith would have safeguarded his financial interests by entering "To Anacreon in Heaven" for copyright, if he really was the composer? and Since he apparently did not copyright the song, does not this absence of a copyright claim argue against his authorship? Why, then, if he was the composer, did he not copyright "To Anacreon in Heaven" in its original form as a song? To ask such questions is very much easier than to answer them to the satisfaction of those who ask them. In themselves these questions are reasonable enough, but they proceed from a faulty premise. If by neglect of copyright entry of "To Anacreon in Heaven" Smith had furnished a glaring exception to a universal rule, then, indeed, but only then would these questions have the force of negative arguments. As a matter of fact—this opinion was recently verified through Miss Constance H. White for the Library of Congress by the officials of Stationers' Hall—copyright entry at Stationers' Hall was never compulsory, and though even many *sheet* songs were entered and certified for copyright, much music was published in England between the years 1770 and 1800 without having been copyrighted at all. This important fact applies not merely to obscure British composers or music publishers, but with equal force to the best known, and it applies also to a good deal of valuable music issued anonymously, as every student of Mr. Barclay Squire's catalogue appreciates. How are we to know at this late date why this or that "good business man" among composers and music publishers neglected to put himself under the protecting wing of the copyright act? To speculate along these lines appears, at least to me, to be futile. Moreover, such speculation projects modern practices into the past with its different practices and against such inapplicable, anachronistic comparison those who dabble in history can not be warned too strongly. To lose their amateurish flavor and to partake of legitimate historical curiosity, questions like the above would have to be amended thus: If Smith was in the habit of copyrighting his music and if he did compose "To Anacreon in Heaven," does it not stand to reason that he would have copyrighted also this song? and If he did not copyright it, does not this

fact, considering his habits in such matters, argue against his authorship? A satisfactory answer to these legitimate questions with their
inferential force can only be given by establishing first Smith's habits
in the matter of copyright claims. Accordingly, the Library of
Congress instructed its London agents to search the Stationers' Hall
records from 1770 to 1800 with special reference to the following
works of John Stafford Smith preceding his Fifth Book of 1799 and
all in our possession:

> A Select collection of catches canons and glees of different kinds . . . com-
> posed by J. S. Smith, London, John Welcker [1780?]
> A Miscellaneous collection of New Songs, catches and glees . . . the whole
> compos'd by John Stafford Smith, London, James Blundell [1780]
> A collection of glees . . . including some . . . which have gained prize
> medals . . . the whole composed by J. S. Smith. London, Welcker [1776?]
> A Collection of Songs of various kinds . . . Composed by John Stafford Smith.
> London, J. Preston [date?]

*We were informed that no copyright entry was found for any of these
works, nor for any other work by John Stafford Smith, except his Fifth
Book!*
Evidently Smith was not in the habit of copyrighting his works.

If he did not consider it necessary to claim copyright in four out
of his five collections, we have no right to find fault with him—fault
belated and based on the inapplicable practice of modern composers—
for having neglected to copyright "To Anacreon in Heaven"! Still
less the right to play out unsound "business" arguments against the
word of a Gentleman of His Majesty's Chapels Royal that he, John
Stafford Smith, was the author (composer) of "To Anacreon in
Heaven," once popular as "The Anacreontic Song"!

Tracing the American history of the air, or rather the history of its
use in America, one runs across these statements in Mr. Salisbury's
"Essay on The Star-Spangled Banner," 1873, page 7:

> I do not discover that it was a favorite when Robert Treat Paine, jr., used its
> measure in his spirited song entitled "Adams and Liberty" [1798].

Page 9:

> After sixteen years, in which the tune of the Anacreontic song was seldom
> heard in this country or in Europe, it was applied to the pathetic verses of Mr. Key.

The second of these statements is nonsensical, the first at least
improbable, because it is now known that the musical intercourse
between England and America was too lively in those days to have
permitted such a well-known air as "To Anacreon in Heaven," published in the most popular collections, to have remained barred from
our shores. The chances are entirely in favor of the possibility that
the song had its votaries here in the seventies or eighties, the more so
as Parke states Sir Richard Hankey, later on president of the Anacreontic Society, to have served in the British army during our war for
independence. Nor would it be at all reasonable to assume that the
"Columbian Anacreontic Society" founded in imitation of the Lon-

don Society in 1795 at New York, the moving spirit of which was for years the great actor-vocalist and bon vivant John Hodgkinson, should not have helped to spread a familiarity with "To Anacreon in Heaven." Indeed, at least one performance of it in public is reasonably certain, namely, when the "Anacreontic Song" was sung by Mr. J. West at a concert at Savannah, Ga., August 19, 1796. However, Mr. Salisbury himself assists in undermining his theory that "To Anacreon in Heaven" was little known in America before it was applied to Key's "pathetic verses." On page 5 of his essay he writes of having seen it in *his* copy of "The Vocal Companion, published in Philadelphia, by Matthew Carey in 1796." It matters little that no copy of this mysterious collection is preserved at the Library of Congress, Boston Public, New York Public, Brown University, Philadelphia Library Company, Pennsylvania Historical Society, Princeton University, American Antiquarian Society; Mr. Salisbury must have seen the song in a copy of some collection in his possession. Then he mentions Robert Treat (scil. Thomas) Paine's spirited "Adams and Liberty" ("Ye Sons of Columbia who bravely have fought") written for and sung to the tune of "To Anacreon in Heaven" at the anniversary of the Massachusetts Charitable Fire Society in Boston on June 1, 1798. A photographic facsimile of this famous song is given here as it was published in the very popular "American Musical Miscellany" of 1798. (Appendix, Plate X.) Mr. Salisbury further mentions Paine's song "Spain" set to the same tune for a Boston festival in honor of the Spanish patriots, January 24, 1809. He also mentions (in footnote, p. 10) a "patriotic offshot" of the Anacreontic song, "perhaps as good as any other commonly known before 1814" [!] which appeared in The New York Remembrancer, Albany, 1802, with the first line "To the Gods who preside o'er the nation below," attributed by the Boston Daily Advertiser, May 1, 1873, to Jonathan Mitchell Sewall, of Portsmouth, N. H.

To these four instances of the early American use of "To Anacreon in Heaven" may be added these in the following collections:

1797. Columbian Songster, New York, p. 136. Song: For the glorious Fourteenth of July. ("The Genius of France from his star begem'd throne.")

1799. Columbian Songster, Wrentham, Mass. Song. 32: Union of the gods.

1799. A Collection of Songs selected from the works of Mr. Charles Dibdin, to which are added the newest and most favorite American Patriotic Songs, Philadelphia.

 p. 315. Boston Patriotic Song [Adams and Liberty].

 p. 326. Our Country's efficiency ("Ye sons of Columbia, determined to keep").

1800. American Songster, Baltimore:

 p. 9. "To Columbia, who gladly reclin'd at her ease . . .

 p. 13. "Ye Sons of Columbia, unite in the cause."

  No tunes are indicated for these two, but the metre plainly suggests "To Anacreon in Heav'n."

 p. 233. "To Anacreon in Heav'n."

1802. Vocal companion, Boston. Song XVI. By J. F. Stanfield, Sunderland. ("Not the fictions of Greece, nor the dreams of old Rome.")

1803. The American Republican Harmonist:
- p. 4. "New Song sung at the celebration of the 4th of July, at Saratoga and Waterford, N. Y. By William Foster" (Brave sons of Columbia, your triumph behold).
- p. 30. Jefferson and Liberty. ("Ye sons of Columbia, who cherish the prize." Text merely altered from Adams and Liberty.)
- p. 105. Song [for the fourth of July, 1803] ("In years which are past, when America fought).
- p. 111. Song. Sung on the 4th of March, at an entertainment given by the American Consul at London. ("Well met, fellow free men! lets cheerfully greet.")
- p. 126. Song for the anniversary festival of the Tammany Society, May 12, 1803. Written by Brother D. E.

1804. 'Nightingale,' selected by Samuel Larkin, Portsmouth.
- p. 69. Adams and Liberty.
- p. 188. To Anacreon in Heaven.

1804. Baltimore Musical Miscellany:
- v. 1, p. 26. Anacreon in Heaven (given in Appendix in facsimile, Pl. XI).
- p. 29. "When Bibo went down to the regions below."
- p. 121. Sons of Columbia [Adams and Liberty].
- v. 2, p. 158. The Social Club.

1811. Musical Repository, Augusta.
- p. 22. Young Bibo. ("For worms when old Bibo prov'd delicate fun.")
- p. 140. Adams and Liberty [without indication of the tune].
- p. 207. Union of the Gods. ("To Columbia, who gladly clined at her ease.")

1813. James J. Wilson, National Song Book, Trenton.
- p. 43. "For the Fourth of July" ("Columbians arise! let the cannon resound.")
- p. 66. "Embargo and Peace" ("When our sky was illuminated by freedom's bright dawn.")
- p. 68. "Union and Liberty." ("Hark! The Trumpet of war from the East sounds alarm.")
- p. 70. "Freedom." ("Of the victory won over tyrany's power.")
- p. 87. "The Fourth of July." ("O'er the forest crowned hills, the rich vallies and streams.")
- p. 88. "Jefferson's Election." Sung by the Americans in London, March 4, 1802. "Well met, fellow freemen! Let's cheerfully greet.")

In addition to these references should be mentioned the very scarce sheet song in possession of the Boston Public Library (reproduced by permission in the Appendix, Plate XII): "Adams and Liberty. The Boston Patriotic Song. Written by Thomas Paine, A. M. ...New York. Printed & Sold by W. Howe, Organ Builder & Importer of all Kinds of Musical Instruments. No. 320 Pearl Street." (This sheet song can not have appeared before 1798 nor after 1799 since we find in the New York City Directory of 1800 "Howe, widow of William, musical store, 320 Pearl St." The date probably is 1798.)

"THE STAR-SPANGLED BANNER"

Opinions differ widely on the merits of "The Star-Spangled Banner" as a national song. Some critics fail to see in Francis Scott Key's inspired lines poetry of more than patriotic value. Some look upon it merely as a flag song, a military song, but not as a national hymn. Some criticize the melody for its excessive range, but others see no defects in "The Star-Spangled Banner" and feel not less enthusiastic over its esthetic merits as a national song than over its sincere patriotic sentiment. This controversy will be decided, whether rightly or wrongly, by the American people regardless of critical analysis, legislative acts, or naïve efforts to create national songs by prize competition. This report does not concern itself at all with such quasi esthetic problems, nor is it here the place to trace the political history of "The Star-Spangled Banner" beyond what is necessary for the understanding of its history as a national song.

Until recently the first, though brief, account of the origin of "The Star-Spangled Banner" was believed to have appeared in the Baltimore American on September 21, 1814, but Mr. John C. Fitzpatrick, of the Manuscript Division of the Library of Congress, found in our volume of the Baltimore Patriot (publishers, Munroe & French), which had not been accessible to me when I wrote my "Report" of 1909, the following account in No. 59, September 20, 1814, the first issue of the paper after its temporary suspension of publication with No. 58, September 10, 1814:

DEFENSE OF FORT M'HENRY.

[The following beautiful and animating effusion, which is destined long to outlast the occasion and outlive the impulse which produced it, has already been extensively circulated. In our first renewal of publication we rejoice in an opportunity to enliven the sketch of an exploit so illustrious, with strains which so fitly celebrate it.]—ED. PAT.

The annexed song was composed under the following circumstances: A gentleman had left Baltimore in a flag of truce for the purpose of getting released from the British fleet a friend of his who had been captured at Marlborough. He went as far as the mouth of the Patuxent, and was not permitted to return lest the intended attack on Baltimore should be disclosed. He was therefore brought up the bay to the mouth of the Patapsco, where the flag vessel was kept under the guns of a frigate, and he was compelled to witness the bombardment of Fort McHenry, which the admiral had boasted that he would carry in a few hours, and that the city must fall. He watched the flag at the fort through the whole day with an anxiety that can be better felt than described, until the night prevented him from seeing it. In the night he watched the bombshells, and at early dawn his eye was again greeted by the proudly waving flag of his country.

This account is followed by the text of Key's poem without special title, but with the indication: "Tune: Anacreon in Heaven." (See Appendix, Plate XIII.) One day later the Baltimore American printed the same historical account, with text of Key's poem and indication of the tune, but without the so curiously prophetic remarks of the editor and without any allusion to previous extensive circulation of account and text.[a]

As this account was printed almost immediately after the events therein described took place, and were in every reader's memory, the newspaper editors, of course, omitted specific dates, but it is a matter of history that the gallant defense of Fort McHenry under Maj. Armistead began on the morning of Tuesday, September 13, and lasted until the early hours of September 14, 1814. The *gentleman* is, of course, Francis Scott Key, and either his own modesty or an editorial whim kept his authorship from the public.

The first detailed and authentic account of the origin of "The Star-Spangled Banner" practically came from Francis Scott Key himself, who narrated it shortly after the British designs on Baltimore failed, to his brother-in-law, Mr. R. B. Taney, subsequently Chief Justice of our Supreme Court. When in 1856 Mr. Henry V. D. Jones edited the "Poems of the Late Francis S. Key, Esq. . . ." (New York, 1857), Chief Justice Taney contributed Key's version from memory, in an introductory "letter . . . narrating the incidents connected with the origin of the song 'The Star-Spangled Banner.'" This interesting narrative has been made the basis of all subsequent accounts. Its substance is this: When, after the battle of Bladensburg, the main body of the British army had passed through the town of Upper Marlborough, some stragglers, who had left the ranks to plunder or from some other motive, made their appearance from time to time, singly or in small squads, and a Dr. Beanes, who had previously been very hospitable to the British officers, "put himself at the head of a small body of citizens to pursue and make prisoners" of the stragglers. Information of this proceeding reached the British and Dr. Beanes was promptly seized. The British "did not seem to regard him, and certainly did not treat him, as a prisoner of war, but as one who had deceived and broken his faith to them." Dr. Beanes was the leading physician of his town and so highly respected that the news of his imprisonment filled his friends with alarm. They

---

[a] Mr. David E. Roberts, of the Library of Congress, had the kindness to verify for me the following facts: The last issue of the Baltimore American (publishers, W. Pechin, G. Dobbin, and Murphy) before suspension was on September 10, 1814, with No. 4762. The first issue after suspension appeared on September 20, 1814, as No. 4766, but this number of September 20, 1814, did *not* contain Key's poem. The Baltimore American printed it on September 21, 1814, but not before. By courtesy of the Maryland Historical Society a facsimile of the Baltimore American text appears in the appendix as Plate XIV.

"hastened to the headquarters of the English army to solicit his release, but it was peremptorily refused," and they were informed that he had been carried as a prisoner on board the fleet. Francis Scott Key happened also to be one of the doctor's intimate friends, and as Mr. Key, just then a volunteer in Maj. Peter's Light Artillery, but a lawyer by profession, was a resident of Georgetown, which means practically Washington, the other friends requested him—

to obtain the sanction of the Government to his going on board the admiral's ship under a flag of truce and endeavoring to procure the release of Dr. Beanes, before the fleet sailed.

. . . Mr. Key readily agreed to undertake the mission in his favor, and the President [Madison] promptly gave his sanction to it. Orders were immediately issued to the vessel usually employed as a cartel [the *Minden*] in the communications with the fleet in the Chesapeake to be made ready without delay; and Mr. John S. Skinner, who was agent for the Government for flags of truce and exchange of prisoners, and who was well known as such to the officers of the fleet, was directed to accompany Mr. Key. And as soon as the arrangements were made, he hastened to Baltimore, where the vessel was, to embark; . . .

We heard nothing from him until the enemy retreated from Baltimore, which, as well as I can now recollect, was a week or ten days after he left us; and we were becoming uneasy about him when, to our great joy, he made his appearance at my house, on his way to join his family.

He told me that he found the British fleet at the mouth of the Potomac, preparing for the expedition against Baltimore. He was courteously received by Admiral Cochrane and the officers of the army, as well as the navy. But when he made known his business his application was received so coldly that he feared he would fail. General Ross and Admiral Cockburn—who accompanied the expedition to Washington—particularly the latter, spoke of Dr. Beanes in very harsh terms, and seemed at first not disposed to release him. It, however, happened, fortunately, that Mr. Skinner carried letters from the wounded British officers left at Bladensburg, and in these letters to their friends on board the fleet they all spoke of the humanity and kindness with which they had been treated after they had fallen into our hands. And after a good deal of conversation and strong representations from Mr. Key as to the character and standing of Dr. Beanes, and of the deep interest which the community in which he lived took in his fate, Gen. Ross said that Dr. Beanes deserved much more punishment than he had received; but that he felt himself bound to make a return for the kindness which had been shown to his wounded officers, whom he had been compelled to leave at Bladensburg; and upon that ground, and that only, he would release him. But Mr. Key was at the same time informed that neither he, nor any one else, would be permitted to leave the fleet for some days, and must be detained until the attack on Baltimore, which was then about to be made, was over. But he was assured that they would make him and Mr. Skinner as comfortable as possible while they detained him. Admiral Cochrane, with whom they dined on the day of their arrival, apoligized for not accommodating them on his own ship, saying that it was crowded already with officers of the army, but that they would be well taken care of in the frigate *Surprise*, commanded by his son, Sir Thomas Cochrane. And to this frigate they were accordingly transferred.

Mr. Key had an interview with Dr. Beanes before General Ross consented to release him. I do not recollect whether he was on board the admiral's ship or the *Surprise*, but I believe it was the former. He found him in the forward part of the ship, among the sailors and soldiers; he had not had a change of clothes from the time he was seized; was constantly treated with indignity by those around him, and no officer would speak to him. He was treated as a culprit, and not as a prisoner of war. And this harsh and humiliating treatment continued until he was placed on board the cartel.

Mr. Key and Mr. Skinner continued on board of the *Surprise*, where they were very kindly treated by Sir Thomas Cochrane, until the fleet reached the Patapsco, and preparations were making for landing the troops. Admiral Cochrane then shifted his flags to the frigate, in order that he might be able to move farther up the river, and superintend in person, the attack by water, on the fort. And Mr. Key and Mr. Skinner were then sent on board their own vessel, with a guard of sailors, or marines, to prevent them from landing. They were permitted to take Dr. Beanes with them and they thought themselves fortunate in being anchored in a position which enabled them to see distinctly the flag of Fort McHenry from the deck of the vessel. He proceeded then with much animation to describe the scene on the night of the bombardment. He and Mr. Skinner remained on deck during the night, watching every shell, from the moment it was fired, until it fell, listening with breathless interest to hear if an explosion followed. While the bombardment continued, it was sufficient proof that the fort had not surrendered. But it suddenly ceased some time before day; and as they had no communication with any of the enemy's ships, they did not know whether the fort had surrendered, or the attack upon it been abandoned. They paced the deck for the residue of the night in painful suspense, watching with intense anxiety for the return of day, and looking every few minutes at their watches, to see how long they must wait for it; and as soon as it dawned, and before it was light enough to see objects at a distance, their glasses were turned to the fort, uncertain whether they should see there the Stars and Stripes, or the flag of the enemy. At length the light came, and they saw that "our flag was still there." And as the day advanced, they discovered, from the movements of the boats between the shore and the fleet, that the troops had been roughly handled, and that many wounded men were carried to the ships. At length he was informed that the attack on Baltimore had failed, and the British army was reembarking, and that he and Mr. Skinner, and Dr. Beanes would be permitted to leave them, and go where they pleased, as soon as the troops were on board, and the fleet ready to sail.

He then told me that, under the excitement of the time, he had written a song, and handed me a printed copy of "The Star-Spangled Banner." When I had read it, and expressed my admiration, I asked him how he found time, in the scenes he had been passing through, to compose such a song? He said he commenced it on the deck of their vessel, in the fervor of the moment, when he saw the enemy hastily retreating to their ships, and looked at the flag he had watched for so anxiously as the morning opened; that he had written some lines, or brief notes that would aid him in calling them to mind, upon the back of a letter which he happened to have in his pocket; and for some of the lines, as he proceeded, he was obliged to rely altogether on his memory; and that he finished it in the boat on his way to the shore, and wrote it out as it now stands, at the hotel, on the night he reached Baltimore, and immediately after he arrived. He said that on the next morning, he took it to Judge Nicholson, to ask him what he thought of it, that he was so much pleased with it, that he immediately sent it to a printer, and directed copies to be struck off in hand-bill form; and that he, Mr. Key, believed it to have been favorably received by the Baltimore public.

Judge Nicholson and Mr. Key, you know, were nearly connected by marriage, Mrs. Key and Mrs. Nicholson being sisters. The judge was a man of cultivated taste, had at one time been distinguished among the leading men in Congress, and was at the period of which I am speaking the Chief Justice of the Baltimore, and one of the Judges of the Court of Appeals, of Maryland.   Notwithstanding his judicial character, which exempted him from military service, he accepted the command of a volunteer company of artillery.   And when the enemy approached, and an attack on the fort was expected, he and his company offered their services to the Government, to assist in its defence.   They were accepted, and formed a part of the garrison, during the bombardment.   The Judge had been relieved from duty, and returned to his family only the night before Mr. Key showed him his song.   And you may easily imagine the feelings with which, at such a moment, he read it, and gave it to the public.   It was, no doubt, as Mr. Key modestly expressed it, favorably received.   *In less than an hour after it was placed in the hands of the printer, it was all over town, and hailed with enthusiasm, and took its place at once as a national song   . . .*[a]

More than 40 years had elapsed since Chief Justice Taney had heard this story for the first time from Francis Scott Key, and though it probably was modified or embellished in course of time, yet in substance it has the earmarks of authenticity.   Exactly for this reason, if for no other, Chief Justice Taney's account furnished the foundation for all further accounts, but it should be noticed that the Chief Justice does not tell us anything beyond how the words came to be written, until struck off in handbill form.   We do not learn when and under what circumstances the broadside was printed, how the poem was wedded to its music, or when and by whom the song was first read or sung.   If certain writers do include such statements in their quotations from Taney's account, they certainly did not read Taney's introductory letter, but most probably copied their quotations from Admiral Preble, who indeed but carelessly attributes such statements to the Chief Justice.   The data not contained in Taney's account had to be supplied by others, and it is very curious that instantly this part of the history of "The Star-Spangled Banner" became confused, whereas Chief Justice Taney's account remained unchallenged except in unimportant points, as for instance, the reasons for Dr. Beanes's arrest.   Under this head Chief Justice Taney was rather vague; not so Mrs. Anna H. Dorsey, who in the Washington Sunday Morning Chronicle added some "lesser facts," which were reprinted in Dawson's Historical Magazine, 1861, volume 5, pages 282–283.   According to Mrs. Dorsey, Dr. William Beanes, the uncle of her mother, was celebrating with copious libations a rumored British defeat at Washington when "three foot-sore, dusty, and weary soldiers made their appearance on the scene in quest of water."   Somewhat under the influence of the excellent punch, Dr. Beanes and his friends made them pris-

---

[a] Had Chief Justice Taney foreseen how easily his words here printed in italics lent themselves to uncritical repetition and paraphrase, I have no doubt that he would have used more conservative language to express his thought and not these words which involve an absolute physical impossibility, and the last words an historical impossibility.

oners of war, and very naturally, the British resented this, to say the least, indiscreet act. This Beanes-Dorsey family tradition is given here for all it is worth, but if correct, then it would be a singular coincidence that an English drinking song called "To Anacreon in Heaven" furnished the melody for a poem which had its root in an event inspired by Bacchus. Indeed Dr. Beanes and his friends might have been voicing their sentiments " to Anacreon in Heaven."

Different is the account written by Mr. F. S. Key Smith for the Republic Magazine, 1908, April, pages 10–20, on "Fort McHenry and the Star-Spangled Banner." According to Mr. Smith, a party of marauding stragglers came into the doctor's garden and intruded themselves upon him and his little company. "Elated over their supposed victory of the day previous, of which the Doctor and his friends had heard nothing," says Mr. Smith, "they were boisterous, disorderly, and insolent, and upon being ordered to leave the premises became threatening. Whereupon, at the instance of Doctor Beanes and his friends, they were arrested by the town authorities and lodged in the Marlborough jail."

This version, too, is quoted here for all it is worth; but it should be noted that throughout this article, dealing elaborately only with the political history of Key's poem, Mr. Smith is conspicuously silent about his authorities, thus preventing critical readers from accepting his statements without skepticism. A case in point is his continuation of Chief Justice Taney's narrative:

> He [Judge Nicholson, also Key's brother-in-law] took it [what Mr. Smith calls "the first complete draft of the song"] to the printing office of Captain Benjamin Edes on North Street near the corner of Baltimore street, but the Captain not having returned from duty with the Twenty-Sixth Maryland Regiment, his office was closed, and Judge Nicholson proceeded to the newspaper office of the Baltimore American and Commercial Daily Advertiser, where the words were set in type by Samuel Sands, an apprentice at the time, but who in later life became associated with Colonel Skinner in the editing and publishing of the American Farmer, the first agricultural paper published in the United States and possibly in the world. Copies of the song were struck off in handbill form, and promiscuously distributed on the street. Catching with popular favor like prairie fire it spread in every direction, was read and discussed, until, in less than an hour, the news was all over the city. *Picked up by a crowd assembled about Captain McCauley's tavern, next to the Holliday Street Theater, where two brothers Charles and Ferdinand Durang, musicians and actors, were stopping, the latter mounted a chair, and rendered it in fine style to a large assemblage.*
>
> *On the evening of the same day that Mr. Charles* [!!] *Durang first sang " The Star Spangled Banner," it was again rendered upon the stage of the Holliday Street Theater by an actress,* and the theater is said to have gained thereby a national reputation. *In less than a week it had reached New Orleans* [!] and was publicly played by a military band, and shortly thereafter was heard in nearly, if not all, the principal cities and towns throughout the country . . .

On March 28, 1911, Mr. Smith published an attractive book under the title "Francis Scott Key. Author of the Star Spangled Banner.

What else he was and who.   By F. S. Key-Smith, Esq." Again Mr. Smith was conspicuously silent about his authorities in the matter of the disputed points here under discussion, but it is interesting to note that Mr. Smith quietly changed the words italicized by me above in the quotation from Mr. Smith's article of 1908 to read, with additions and omissions, in his book of 1911, as follows:

> *Picked up by a crowd* of soldiers *assembled,* some accounts put it *about Captain McCauley's tavern, next to the Holiday-Street Theater* others have it around their tents on the out-skirts of the city [NB. the omission], *Ferdinand Durang,* a musician, adapted the words to the old tune of "Anacreon in Heaven," and, *mounting a chair, rendered it in fine style.* [NB. the omission]
>
> *On the evening of the same day* [NB. the omission] *it was again rendered . . .* [same as in 1908]   *In* about a fortnight [N. B. the difference] *it had reached New Orleans . . .* [same as in 1908]

Inconsistencies like these illustrate glaringly the necessity of reference in historical work to the author's sources, whether they be original manuscripts in his possession or what not.   Such references can be made even in magazine articles unobtrusively, with just a modicum of literary skill, and without the cumbersome apparatus of legal articles.   It is the duty of the would-be historian to record his "authorities" of his own accord and in the proper place, and not to wait for the critics to ring his door bell.   Otherwise, the absence of "authorities" from disputed points of historical narrative will prompt even an impartially inclined but sceptical reviewer to call accounts like the above "merely the hastily concocted and uncritically diluted essence of previous articles, including that by Taney," as I did in my "Report" of 1909.   To this severe criticism Mr. Smith quite naturally took offence in letters addressed to me and to the Librarian of Congress on March 3, 1911, claiming that his account had been based on an "original manuscript in his possession," the nature of which Mr. Smith disclosed neither in his letters nor in his book.   Notwithstanding this "original manuscript," Mr. Smith, as is shown above, found himself obliged in his book of 1911 to contradict his article of 1908 as soon as he reached the points here under discussion.   The more reason, it would seem to me, to have disclosed unasked the nature and authenticity of this manuscript.   Moreover, in itself, no "original manuscript" has any standing in a court of historical inquiry, unless the contents of the manuscript successfully resist critical pressure.

To his article of 1908, so far as it concerns us here, Mr. Smith added a quotation from the same letter by Samuel Sands, which will be presently quoted by me, some remarks about the flag that inspired Francis Scott Key and this reference to the "Report" of 1909:

> The accuracy of the version herein given of the arrest of Dr. Beans, as well as the statements that Samuel Sands first set the words of the Star Spangled Banner in type, seems to be questioned by Oscar George Theodore Sonneck . . . It

would appear that he prefers to accept the version . . . [follows the Beans-Dorsey family tradition, with comment] . . . As for the statement that Mr. Sands first set the song in type, his own letter, herein published . . . is a sufficient justification and, it is submitted, better evidence than the claims of friends and descendants of others anxious to gain some share in the honor connected with writing and publishing the National Anthem. It is most unfortunate that such errors should appear in a publication bearing the official stamp of our Government.

From "seems to be questioned" to "such errors" is a rather abrupt step. Mr. Smith is challenged to point out a single statement in the "Report" of 1909 which would justify him in claiming that I favored one version of the Dr. Beans episode as against the others. He is further challenged to point out where I questioned the accuracy of the statement that Samuel Sands first set the words of "The Star-Spangled Banner" in type.[a] Finally, it may interest Mr. Smith to know, as it may others, that the United States officially is still without a national anthem. True, the Army and Navy use "The Star-Spangled Banner" officially. True, also, that the majority of our people seem to favor and to use "The Star-Spangled Banner" on patriotic occasions; but it is also true that as yet, at the date of writing, the United States has *not* officially, through its Representatives in Congress, designated "The Star-Spangled Banner" or any other of our national songs as "*the* national anthem." [b]

In the following no attempt will be made to dissect or even pay much attention to the second-hand compilations from original sources, no matter how spirited or otherwise attractive they may be.

One C. D., in the Historical Magazine of 1864, volume 8, pages 347–348, has this to say:

> One of your correspondents inquires in what form the song of the Star Spangled Banner was first printed. I think that in the History of the Philadelphia Stage you will find that subject clearly explained. The song was first printed and put

---

[a] On p. 29–31 of my "Report" (now p. 85–88) I refuted Preble's assumption that Samuel Sands set the elaborate broadside fac-similed by Dielman, therewith proving that it was the other broadside which Sands set up in type. Mr. Smith apparently did not notice this distinction.

[b] In the House of Representatives, January 30, 1913, Mr. Jefferson M. Levy introduced the following joint resolution [H. J. Res. 391, 62d Congress, 3d Session]; which was referred to the Committee on the Judiciary and ordered to be printed:

Joint resolution recognizing "The Star-Spangled Banner" as the official anthem of the United States of America.

Resolved by the Senate and House of Representatives of the United States of America in Congress assembled, That on and after the passage of this resolution "The Star-Spangled Banner" shall be recognized as the official anthem of the United States of America.

SEC. 2. That whenever "The Star-Spangled Banner" is played on any occasion at any public place where persons belonging to any branch of the Government service are present they will stand at attention, and all other citizens will stand, such positions. being retained until the last note of "The Star-Spangled Banner."

The clerk of the Judiciary Committee informed us on November 13, 1913, and again on March 18, 1914, that no further action had been taken.

upon the press by Captain Edes, of Baltimore, who belonged to Colonel Long's Twenty-seventh Regiment of militia. He kept his printing office at the corner of Baltimore and Gay Streets. It was given him by the author, Mr. Key, of Washington, in its amended form, after the battle of North Point, about the latter end of September, 1814. The original draft, with its interlineations and amendatory erasures, etc., was purchased by the late Gen. George Keim, of Reading, and I suppose his heirs have it now. It was printed on a small piece of paper in the style of our old ballads that were wont to be hawked about the streets in days of yore. It was first sung by about twenty volunteer soldiers in front of the Holliday Street Theater, who used to congregate at the adjoining tavern to get their early mint juleps. Ben. Edes brought it round to them on one of those libating mornings or matinees. I was one of the group. My brother sang it. We all formed the chorus. This is its history . . .

The reference to the History of the Philadelphia Stage and to "my brother" immediately implies the identity of this C. D. with Charles Durang, brother of Ferdinand Durang (both actors), and joint author, or, rather, editor, of his father John's History of the Philadelphia Stage, published serially in the Philadelphia Sunday Dispatch, 1854–55. Consequently we have here the (unfortunately not very accurate) testimony of a contemporary earwitness. A few years later, in 1867, Col. John L. Warner read before the Pennsylvania Historical Society a paper on "The origin of the American national anthem called The Star-Spangled Banner," and this paper was printed in the Historical Magazine, 1867, Volume II, pages 279–280. As will be seen from the following quotation, it does not contradict Charles Durang's account, but merely supplements it. Says Col. Warner:

It was first sung when fresh from his [Capt. Benjamin Edes!] press, at a small frame one-story house, occupied as a tavern next to the Holiday Street Theatre.

This tavern had long been kept by the widow Berling, and then by a Col. MacConkey, a house where the players "most did congregate," with the quid nuncs of that day, to do honor to, and to prepare for, the daily military drills in Gay Street (for every able man was then a soldier); and here came, also, Capt. Benjamin Edes, of the Twenty-seventh Regiment; Captain Long and Captain Thomas Warner, of the Thirty-ninth Regiment; and Major Frailey. Warner was a silversmith of good repute in that neighborhood.

It was the latter end of September, 1814, when a lot of the young volunteer defenders of the Monumental City were thus assembled. Captain Edes and Captain Thomas Warner came early along one morning and forthwith called the group (quite merry with the British defeat) to order, to listen to a patriotic song which the former had just struck off at his press. He then read it to all the young volunteers there assembled, who greeted each verse with hearty shouts. It was then suggested that it should be sung; but who was able to sing it? Ferdinand Durang, who was a soldier in the cause and known to be a vocalist, being among the group, was assigned the task of vocalising this truly inspired patriotic hymn of the lamented Key. The old air of "Anacreon in Heaven" had been adapted to it by the author, and Mr. Edes was desired so to print it on the top of the ballad.

Its solemn melody and impressive notes seem naturally allied to the poetry, and speak emphatically the musical taste and judgment of Mr. Key. Ferdinand Durang mounted an old-fashioned rush-bottomed chair, and sang this admirable national song for the first time in our Union, the chorus to each verse being re-echoed by those present with infinite harmony of voices. It was thus sung several times during the morning. When the theater was opened by Warren and Wood, it was sung nightly, after the play, by Paddy McFarland and the company.

So far the historian would have plain sailing, but his troubles begin with an article written for Harper's Magazine, 1871, volume 43, pages 254–258, by Mrs. Nellie Eyster, as appears from the printed index. Under the title of "The Star-Spangled Banner: An hour with an octogenarian," she reports an interview held on November 20, 1870, with Mr. Hendon, of Frederick, Md., who knew Francis Scott Key personally as a boy and who moved in 1809 to Lancaster, Pa., whence both the Durangs hailed. Together with Charles and Ferdinand Durang he belonged to the Pennsylvania Volunteer Militia, which on August 1, 1814, left Harrisburg in defense of Baltimore, but, remembers Mr. Hendon, they "marched to the seat of war three days after the battle had been won," and with special reference to the defense of Fort McHenry he "was chafing like a caged tiger because [he] was not in it." He further says that "they remained upon Gallows Hill, near Baltimore, for three months, daily waiting for an enemy that never came. Then, for the first time since leaving York [Pa.], [they] took breathing time and looked about for amusement." Follows what Admiral George Henry Preble called a more fanciful version than Warner's account when he copied Mr. Hendon's words for a footnote (p. 494) in the chapter on "Our National Songs" (pp. 490–511) in the first edition (Albany, 1872) of his industrious and popular compilation, Our Flag:

"Have you heard Francis Key's poem?" said one of our men, coming in one evening, as we lay scattered over the green hill near the captain's marquee. It was a rude copy, and written in a scrawl which Horace Greeley might have mistaken for his own. He read it aloud, once, twice, three times, until the entire division seemed electrified by its pathetic eloquence.

An idea seized Ferd. Durang. Hunting up a volume of flute music, which was in somebody's tent, he impatiently whistled snatches of tune after tune, just as they caught his quick eye. One, called "Anacreon in Heaven," (I have played it often for it was in my book that he found it), struck his fancy and riveted his attention. Note after note fell from his puckered lips until, with a leap and shout, he exclaimed "Boys, I've hit it!" and fitting the tune to the words, they sang out for the first time the song of the Star-Spangled Banner. How the men shouted and clapped, for never was there a wedding of poetry to music made under such inspiring influences! Getting a brief furlough, the brothers [!!] sang it in public soon after . . .

In the second edition of his work (1880), then called History of the Flag of the United States of America, Admiral Preble reprinted this *fanciful* story, together with the Charles Durang and Col. Warner account, but again without the slightest attempt at critical comparison and apparently without noticing that we do not have to deal here with more or less fanciful differences, but with reminiscent accounts that exclude each other. What subsequent writers contributed in this vein to the literature on "The Star-Spangled Banner" may be disregarded, since they merely paraphrased with more or less accuracy what they found in Preble or in his sources, as, for instance, when one writer in the American Historical Record, 1873, volume 2, pages 24–25, carelessly mentions Charles instead of Ferdinand Durang as the first singer of "The Star-Spangled Banner." However, a belated version with fanciful variations of the main theme should be noticed, as it was printed some time in 1897 in the Philadelphia Ledger and from there reprinted in substance in the Iowa Historical Record, July, 1897, page 144. According to this, "the second day after the words were written, Ferdinand Durang was rummaging in his trunk in a tavern in Baltimore, where he had his baggage, for music to suit the words, and finally selected that of 'Anacreon in Heaven.' By the time he had sung the third verse, in trying the music to the words, the little tavern was full of people, who spontaneously joined in the chorus. The company was soon joined by the author of the words, Francis Scott Key, to whom the tune was submitted for approval, who also took up the refrain of the chorus, thus indorsing the music. A few nights afterward 'The Star-Spangled Banner' being called for by the audience at the Holliday Street Theater, in Baltimore, Ferdinand Durang sang it from the stage. Durang died in New York in 1832. Durang had a brother, Charles, also a soldier in the 'Blues,' who was likewise an actor, who died in Philadelphia in 1875. . . ."

That to Ferdinand Durang belongs the honor of having first sung Key's poem is unanimously asserted (except by those who confuse him with his brother Charles), but it remains an open question when and where he might so have done. On this point the two earwitnesses, Charles Durang and Mr. Hendon, disagree. According to the reminiscences of the latter, the event must have happened at least three months after September 14 in camp on Gallows Hill near Baltimore. Now, it has already been mentioned that the brief account of the circumstances leading to the writing of Key's poem printed in the Baltimore Patriot on September 20, preceded the full text of the poem under the heading "Defence of Fort M'Henry" with the remark "Tune: Anacreon in Heaven." It may be that Mr. Hendon heard Ferdinand Durang sing the hymn in camp after September 20, but it stands to reason that at least as early as September 20 other vocally inclined readers of the Baltimore Patriot enjoyed the combination of Key's "Defence of Fort M'Henry," and the tune "To Anacreon in Heaven." If we possessed no other contemporary evidence, Ferdinand Durang's claims would rest upon very shaky grounds indeed, nor is the rest of Mr. Hendon's story at all of a nature as to inspire reliance upon his memory.   Mr. Elson in his "National Music of America" (p. 202) bluntly expressed his suspicion to the effect that "never was a bolder or more fantastical claim set up in musical history," and every musician will agree with him that the "puckered lips" and the frantic hunt for a suitable tune in a volume of flute music is sheer journalistic nonsense, which verdict applies also to the Philadelphia Ledger account.   And his hunt for a melody happened three months after the tune, with which the words were to keep company, had been publicly announced!

The suspicious character of Mr. Hendon's long-distance reminiscences leaves those of Charles Durang to stand on their own merits, but unfortunately they do not help us in fixing the exact date of the first performance of "The Star-Spangled Banner."   Charles Durang merely remembered having been one of the chorus when his brother Ferdinand and about twenty volunteer soldiers who used to congregate at the adjoining tavern in the morning first sang the song after Benj. Edes brought it round to them on *one* of those libating mornings.   This may have been the morning of September 15, when Samuel Sands, the apprentice, is popularly supposed to have set the poem as a broadside, or any other morning, including a morning after September 20, when the poem had appeared with indication of the tune in the Baltimore Patriot.   Nor is Col. Warner's account, who perhaps was a descendant of Capt. Thomas Warner, which possibility would give his account the strength of a family tradition, more explicit on this point.   *At* this tavern, it being a southern September morning, may mean practically the same as in Charles Durang's version, in front of the adjoining Holliday Street Theater. There Capt. Edes, in company of Capt. Thomas Warner, is said to have called the attention of the group of volunteers "to a patriotic song which [he] had *just* struck off at his press."   Consequently, neither Durang nor Warner substantiate the popular version that Ferdinand Durang sang "The Star-Spangled Banner" for the first time on September 15, 1814.   Nor do they even substantiate the frequently accepted story that the broadside was struck off Edes's press [from which it was not struck off at all] on September 15! Indeed, not even Key-Taney's report: "Judge Nicholson . . . immediately sent it [the manuscript] to a printer, and directed copies to be struck off in hand-bill form," necessarily implies the conclusion that they were struck off on the morning of September 15.   At any rate, the story that Key's poem was taken to a printer, set as a broadside, distributed about town, read, discussed, sung with great gusto, etc., and all this on the morning of September 15, 1814, belongs to the realm of unwholesome historical fiction!

On the evening of September 15 "The Star-Spangled Banner," says Mr. F. S. Key Smith, was "rendered upon the stage of the

Holliday Street Theater by an actress." Also Ferdinand Durang is mentioned in this connection by some writers, and others proffer other names. What are the facts? In the first place, the suspicions of the historians should have been aroused by the observation that the actor-manager, Wood, in his autobiography does not mention any theatrical performances at Baltimore in September, 1814. In the second place, if they had consulted the Baltimore papers of that period, such as the Federal Gazette, Baltimore Patriot, Baltimore American—none of which was published, by the way, by Benjamin Edes!—they would have found no theatrical performances announced in September, 1814, at all, but they would have found a notice in the Federal Gazette, September 20, to the effect that "about 600 Pennsylvania troops arrived yesterday," among them a Lancaster company, apparently the very militia troops to which Ferdinand Durang belonged. Not only this, the historians would further have found from the same source that the *theater was not opened until October 12, 1814.* No reference to "The Star-Spangled Banner" appears in the announcements of this evening or of the benefit performance on October 14 "to aid the fund for the defense of the city," unless hidden away on the benefit program as "a patriotic epilogue by Mrs. Mason." On this evening Ferdinand Durang *did* appear—dancing a "military hornpipe." With a little patience the historians at last would have found in the announcement of the historical play "Count Benyowski" for Wednesday evening, October 19, 1814 (in the Baltimore American appears October 15 as a misprint), the following lines, which at last shed the light of fact on the whole matter:

> After the play, Mr. Harding [the Federal Gazette spells the name Hardinge] will sing a much admired *New Song*, written by a gentleman of Maryland, in commemoration of the GALLANT DEFENSE OF FORT M'HENRY, called, THE STAR-SPANGLED BANNER. . . .

The rather immaterial question of whether or not and when and where Ferdinand Durang possibly sang "The Star-Spangled Banner" for the first time leads up to the much more important question: How came the tune of "To Anacreon in Heaven," and no other, to be wedded to Key's poem? Chief Justice Taney, as anybody can see and as all should have seen before rushing into print with their stories, is absolutely silent on this point. So is Charles Durang. Col. Warner says:

> The old air of Anacreon in Heaven *had been adapted to it by the author*, and Mr. Edes was desired so to print it on to the top of the ballad.

The most reliable reports, therefore, do not mention Ferdinand Durang at all in this connection. He figures as musical godfather to "The Star-Spangled Banner" in the journalistic reports only and under rather suspicious circumstances. However, there exists

another and different version. Mrs. Rebecca Lloyd Shippen, of
Baltimore, a granddaughter of Judge Joseph Hopper Nicholson and
a greatniece of Francis Scott Key, contributed to the Pennsylvania
Magazine of History and Biography, 1901–2, volume 25, pages 427–
428, an article on "The original manuscript of The Star-Spangled
Banner," of which more will have to be said further on.   In this
article we read:

> Judge Nicholson wrote a little piece that appears at the heading of the lines,
> above which he also wrote the name of the tune "Anacreon in Heaven"—a tune
> which Mrs. Charles Howard, the daughter of Francis Scott Key, told me was a
> common one at that day—and Judge Nicholson, being a musician among his
> other accomplishments and something of a poet, no doubt took but a few minutes
> to see that the lines given him by Francis Scott Key could be sung to that tune,
> and, in all haste to give the lines as a song to the public, he thus marked it.   I
> possess this rare original manuscript, kept carefully folded by his wife, Rebecca
> Lloyd Nicholson, and taken from her private papers by myself [Mrs. Shippen]
> and framed.

Judge Nicholson's part in the history of "The Star-Spangled Banner" was narrated in substantially the same manner in editorial foot-
notes to an article on "The Star-Spangled Banner" written by
Mrs. Shippen for the Pennsylvania Magazine of History and Biography, 1898–99, volume 22, pages 321–325, and similar to Taney's
version.   It follows that the editor was either inspired by Mrs.
Shippen or Mrs. Shippen by the editor.   Careful reading of this particular part of the article implies that we do not have to face here
strictly contemporary evidence.   Waiving aside for the present some
doubts as to the accuracy of the story as quoted above, the main
contention appears to be that Judge Nicholson supplied the tune.
Light is shed on the whole matter by the history of the tune "To
Anacreon in Heaven" in England and America investigated in the
preceding pages.

The summary there given of publications of "To Anacreon in
Heaven" was not intended as an exhaustive attempt to trace the
tune "To Anacreon in Heaven" in early American song publications,
but merely to prove and to corroborate by facts that "the tune was
a common one at that day" in America, as Francis Scott Key's own
daughter, Mrs. Howard, told Mrs. Shippen.

We have some further contemporary evidence in this communication sent by Mr. Charles V. Hagner to the American Historical
Record, 1873, volume 2, page 129:

> At the time it was written by Mr. Key, during the attack on Fort McHenry,
> Sept., 1814, there was a very popular and fashionable new song in vogue, viz:
> "To Anacreon in Heaven," every one who could sing seemed to be singing it.
> The writer of this was at the time (Sept., 1814), one of some three to four thou-
> sand men composing the advance Light Brigade, chiefly volunteers from Phila-
> delphia, under the command of General John Cadwalader, then encamped in
> the State of Delaware.   In the evenings before tattoo, many of the men would
> assemble in squads and sing this song, hundreds joining in the chorus.   Mr.
> Key must have caught the infection and adapted his words to the same air.

Francis Scott Key simply can not have escaped "To Anacreon in Heaven"! Indeed so common was the tune that, after Thomas Paine had set the example with his "Adams and Liberty," the music and the rather involved form and meter of "To Anacreon in Heaven" were adopted as *standards* by poetically inclined patriots. This historical fact applies with all its force to Francis Scott Key. The form and meter of "To Anacreon in Heaven," "Adams and Liberty," and "The Star-Spangled Banner" are practically the same, as the juxtaposition of the first stanza will prove, if such proof be necessary.

TO ANACREON IN HEAVEN.

To Anacreon in heaven, where he sat in full glee,
    A few sons of Harmony sent a petition,
That he their inspirer and patron would be,
    When this answer arrived from the jolly old Grecian:
        "Voice, fiddle, and flute,
        "No longer be mute,
"I'll lend ye my name, and inspire ye to boot:
    "And besides, I'll instruct you, like me, to entwine
    "The myrtle of Venus with Bacchus's vine."

THE STAR-SPANGLED BANNER.

O say, can you see by the dawn's early light,
    What so proudly we hailed at the twilight's last gleaming?
Whose broad stripes and bright stars through the perilous fight,
    O'er the ramparts we watched, were so gallantly streaming!
        And the rocket's red glare,
        The bombs bursting in air
Gave proof through the night that our flag was still there;
    O say, does that star-spangled banner yet wave
    O'er the land of the free and the home of the brave?

It is absurd to think that any poetically inclined patriot of those days like Key on the spur of the moment could have set himself to writing a poem of such involved meter and peculiar form as his is without consciously or unconsciously using a model. It is equally absurd under the circumstances to believe any story, tradition, or anecdote from whatever source to the effect that others, with more or less *difficulty*, supplied a tune which fits the words almost more smoothly than does John Stafford Smith's air the Anacreontic text of Ralph Tomlinson. Internal evidence proves that Francis Scott Key, when his imagination took fire from the bombardment of Fort McHenry, had either the meter and form of the words or words and air of "To Anacreon in Heaven" or one of its American offshoots in mind as a scaffold. If this be now taken for granted, two possibilities offer themselves: First, Key wrote his inspired lines as a poem without anticipating its musical use. When shortly afterwards a desire was felt to sing his poem, the identity of poetic meter and form of both poems necessarily, and, as it were, automatically, suggested to

Key himself or any other person of culture the air of "To Anacreon in Heaven." The second possibility is that Key did anticipate the musical possibilities of his poem and intended it as a song to be sung. In that case the fact, as will be seen, that his so-called original manuscript does not contain any indication of the tune may be explained by assuming that Key, very much like the editor of the American Songster, Baltimore (1800), considered it unnecessary to mention what was self-evident to him as the author. Col. Warner's statement that "The old air of 'Anacreon in Heaven' had been adapted to it [the poem] by the author" seems to approach the truth, though if a very fine distinction were to be made we should rather say that the poem was adapted by the author to one of the then current poetic mates of the old air "To Anacreon in Heaven." The first possibility is really the more plausible in view of what Mr. W. U. Hensel, Lancaster, Pa., wrote me under date of March 10, 1910:

> . . . I believe, however, that you have fallen into a misapprehension as to the likelihood of Key having had in his mind and memory the air of "To Anacreon in Heaven." I doubt whether Key knew enough about music to carry any air in his mind. You no doubt have access to the files of the [Philadelphia] Press in the National Library, and you may be interested to know upon the authority of his immediate relatives that I said in my article [Aug. 1, 1881, on Key's early poetry]: Whatever the merits of its composition, it was a matter of little concern to its author. Inclined as he was to rhythmical expression of his fancies he had an ignorance of musical composition that would be utterly inconceivable if it were not, by a most remarkable illustration of the law of heredity made plain in the case of some of his descendants. He could not tell one tune from another. Old Hundred, Yankee Doodle, Hail Columbia, and the Star-Spangled Banner were entirely undistinguishable to the ear of Francis Scott Key. Upon the occasion of the visit to Tuscaloosa, before referred to, he was serenaded, and the local band naturally played the music of his famous song. To the great astonishment and amusement of the gentlemen about him, he innocently remarked that "it was a pretty air," densely ignorant of the tune they were playing. A daughter inherited the same lack of musical aptitude and her daughter, in turn; and now, in the fourth generation, a great-granddaughter of the author of the Star-Spangled Banner has vainly tried for years to accomplish enough musical knowledge to know that tune when it is played.

Even if literally true, this entertaining bit of information would not affect the substance of my argument. I am not claiming that Key must have had in his mind and memory the *music* of the air of "To Anacreon in Heaven." Even if Key had been absolutely deaf and not merely tone-deaf, it was but necessary for him or one of his associates to have in mind and memory the *name* of the air that was generally sung to patriotic songs in the uncommon meter of Key's poem. If Francis Scott Key was so unmusical that he did not even consider the possibility of singing his poem (which, like hundreds of other patriotic poems, would probably have died a natural death without the preserving power of music) not so Judge Nicholson.

He was a "musician and something of a poet," so his granddaughter informed us; I therefore think that her view of the matter is absolutely correct—provided that Key himself did not propose the tune of "To Anacreon in Heaven," or any of its then current American equivalents—if she says:

> Judge Nicholson . . . no doubt took but a few minutes to see that the lines given him by Francis Scott Key could be sung to that tune, and, in all haste to give the lines as a song to the public, he thus marked it.

Whether or not he really thus marked Key's *manuscript* is immaterial, but the really noteworthy fact appears to be that perhaps "The Star-Spangled Banner" owes as much of its popularity to its musically cultured *press agent*, Judge Joseph Hopper Nicholson, as to its possibly unmusical author Francis Scott Key.

Finally an account deserves to be reprinted here in part, because it mentioned the person who set Key's poem in type, though otherwise the lines quoted are not overly accurate, as the reader of the Taney letter will notice. It appeared in the Baltimore American on September 12, 1872, together with a reprint of the article, etc., of September 21, 1814, and reads in part:

> We have placed at the head of this article this now immortal national song just as it first [incorrect; this honor belongs, as was seen, to the Baltimore Patriot] saw the light in print fifty-eight years ago . . . This song, as the form in which it is given shows, was published anonymously. The poet, Francis Scott Key, was too modest to announce himself, and it was some time after its appearance that he became known as its author. . . . Mr. Skinner chanced to meet Mr. Key on the flag-of-truce boat, obtained from him a copy of his song, and he furnished the manuscript to "The American" after the fight was over. It was at once put in type and published. It was also printed in slips and extensively circulated. The "printer's boy," then employed in the office of "The American," who put this song in type, survives in full vigor, our respected friend, the editor and publisher of the "American Farmer," Samuel Sands, Esq.

Fortunately the facts, as recollected by him, have been narrated by Mr. Samuel Sands himself in a letter written under date of January 1, 1877, from the office of the American Farmer to Gen. Brantz Mayer. Mr. John T. Loomis of the firm of W. H. Lowdermilk & Co., Washington, D. C., in 1910 kindly gave me access to this very long but very interesting letter and permission to quote the following for my purposes. Mr. Sands tells the general that he takes the earliest opportunity of giving "a statement of my recollections and impressions of the participation I had in the promulgation of the original copy of our great national song, the Star-Spangled Banner." Previously, he says, he had given sundry items to the editor of the Baltimore American for "the centennial edition of the paper," also, he believed, to Col. Scharff for his chronicles of Baltimore, and more recently, in June, 1874, had printed in the American Farmer a

more detailed account.   Follows an introductory historical narrative based on Taney's letter and remarks on the military quarters
of the "citizen soldiers," mostly from Baltimore, "upon Louden-
slagers Hill, just eastward of the city borders."   Sands then continues:

> Whilst thus located, Mr. Thos. Murphy, one of the members of Capt. Aisquith's
> First Baltimore Sharp Shooters, obtained leave of absence, and returned to the
> city, and again opened the counting room of the American which with all the other
> newspapers of the day, had suspended publication for the time being, the editors,
> journeymen, and apprentices able to bear arms being in the military service.
> According to the best of my recollection I was the only one belonging to the
> printing office that was left who was not in the military service; being then but
> fourteen years of age, and not capable of bearing arms, I whiled away the time
> during the suspense of the invasion in looking after the office and in occasional
> visits to the "boys" at the entrenchments.   After Mr. Murphy's return, the manu-
> script copy of the song was brought to the office—I always had the impression
> that Mr. John S. Skinner brought it, but I never so stated it as a fact, for I had
> no proof thereof, but it was a mere idea and I never considered it of sufficient im-
> portance to make inquiry upon the subject from my old and valued friend, Mr.
> Murphy, or from Mr. Skinner, who was subsequently engaged with me in the
> editing of my farm journal and who was the founder thereof—but the letter of
> Judge Taney alluded to above, proves that I was mistaken in that matter—
> Mr. Skinner was a cartel agent for our Government in its intercourse with the
> British fleet in our Bay and I took up the impression that he on his return from
> the fleet had brought from Mr. Key the manuscript, but Judge Taney gives the
> particulars of the examination and copying of the song, in this city, by Judge
> Nicholson and Mr. Key, and remarks that one of these gentlemen took it to the
> printers.
> When it was brought up to the printing office my impression is, and ever has
> been, that I was the only one of those belonging to the establishment who was
> on hand, and that it was put in type and what the printers call "galley proofs"
> were struck off previous to the renewal of the publication of this paper, and it
> may be and probably was the case that from one of these proof slips handbills
> were printed and circulated through the city.
> This is simply all the part which I had in the transaction alluded to.   Although
> the song obtained celebrity in a little time after it was first presented to the world,
> yet the unimportant and very secondary consideration as to who first printed
> and issued it was never mooted for probably fifty years thereafter when I was
> called upon by sundry persons to give my recollections upon the subject which
> called forth the responses in the several publications alluded to already.
> At the time I put the song in type I was an apprentice in the office of the Balti-
> more American and lived in the family of Mr. Murphy. . . .

One of the popular legends is that Key's poem with its music
spread like wildfire beyond Baltimore, and in a short time became
a national song.   The popular mind seems to consider it a blemish, a
reflection on the intrinsic merits of a song (or any other work of art)
if it does not obtain immediate popularity, and writers who cater
to the tastes and prejudices of the multitude do not hesitate to
amputate the facts accordingly.   "The Star-Spangled Banner"
rather gains than loses in merit if the silly anecdotes of its wildfire

progress are not heeded, and if we adhere to what is still common knowledge among the older generations, namely, that "The Star-Spangled Banner" was not rushed to the front of our national songs until the Civil War.   Before that time its progress as a national song had been steady, but comparatively slow, as anybody may see who follows its career through the American song collections.   This statement in no wise interferes with the fact that Francis Scott Key put it too modestly if he "believed it to have been favorably received by the Baltimore public."   His poem unquestionably soon aroused patriotic interest outside of Baltimore.   For instance, The Analectic Magazine, Philadelphia, 1814, volume 4, November number, page 433 (I owe this reference to Mr. Charles E. Gannon, of Washington, D. C.), printed Key's poem and the original historical note together with these significant introductory remarks:

> These lines have been already published in several of our newspapers; they may still, however, be new to many of our readers.   Besides, we think that their merit entitles them to preservation in some more permanent form than the columns of a daily paper.

How Key's poem, originally written without a title, was beginning to gain ground under the name of "The Star-Spangled Banner" is illustrated by this advertisement, reprinted from the Washington National Intelligencer, January 6, 1815, in the University Musical Encyclopedia, 1911, Volume II:

> STAR SPANGLED BANNER and YE SEAMEN OF COLUMBIA.—Two favorite patriotic songs, this day received and for sale by Richard & Mallory, Bridge Street, Georgetown.

By whom the songs were published and where I do not know, never having seen a copy.   From the wording of the advertisement I infer that perhaps these publications were not broadsides of the customary kind, with mere indication of the tune, but music sheets. In that case, the advertised publication may have been the first appearance in print of Key's poem and Smith's air under the title of "The Star-Spangled Banner."

It would be quite possible to trace with infinite patience the progress of "The Star-Spangled Banner" through the American song collections, but this report hardly calls for such a laborious undertaking.   However, to illustrate the point raised above, one would find that the text of "The Star-Spangled Banner" appears in such songsters as The American Songster, New York, n. d.; New American Songster, Philadelphia, 1817; Bird of Birds, New York, 1818; The Star-Spangled Banner, Wilmington, 1816; The Songster's Magazine, New York, 1820; American Naval and Patriotic Songster, Baltimore, 1831; but not in such as The Songster's Companion, Brattleborough, Vt., 1815; The Songster's Miscellany, Philadelphia, 1817; The Songster's Museum, Hartford, 1826.   In other words, 20 years after its conception Key's "Star-Spangled Banner" was not yet so generally accepted as a national song as to necessitate insertion in *every* songster.

Furthermore, no publication of "The Star-Spangled Banner" appears among the songs deposited for copyright in the several district courts during the years 1819 to 1844 and preserved at the Library of Congress. Unfortunately not *all* copyright deposits have been thus preserved. Nevertheless the fact of absence is suggestive, as is the fact that of our 89 school songbooks published in America between 1834 and 1860 and classified as school songbooks in the Library of Congress only 15 include the "Star-Spangled Banner." The two earliest appearances in our school songbooks are in Johnson and Osgood's Normal Song Book, Boston, 1851 (deposited January 15, 1852), and in Benjamin and Woodbury's New York Normal School Song Book, 1851 (deposited April 12, 1851). In this it forms No. 12 (the last) of part first of " America. Represented in the form of a juvenile oratorio" (compare Appendix, Plate XX). The second part of this patriotic pasticcio concludes with "Hail Columbia," and it is quite obvious from an examination of these 89 school songbooks that "Hail Columbia" and "America," even the "Marseilles Hymn" interested the compilers more than did "The Star-Spangled Banner." As Plate XXI the reader will find in Appendix a facsimile of the "Star-Spangled Banner" as it appears in "Fillmore's New Nightingale; or Normal School Singer . . . on a mathematically constructed plan of notation," Cincinnati, 1857. Not less curious is the version in "buckwheat notes" or "patent notes" in Smith and Ruby's The Vocalist's Pocket Companion, Chambersburg (ᶜ1839), facsimiled on Plate XXII. No earlier dated edition of "The Star-Spangled Banner" for part-song purposes has so far been found in the Library of Congress. It seems to antedate our numerous songbooks for "singing classes," "musical conventions," etc., but with its queer notation offers not half so comical an appearance as the version in Suffern's The Excelsior, Cincinnati, 1862, which presents "The Star-Spangled Banner" with a regular tum-ta-ta, tum-ta-ta waltz accompaniment.

If the idea should prevail that at least the "singing class" type of songbooks generally included "The Star-Spangled Banner," I am inclined to disagree. At any rate, the "Star-Spangled Banner" will *not* be found in such popular songbooks as B. F. Baker's The Philharmonic, 1847; A. D. Fillmore's The Universal Musician, 1850; Ch. Jarvis's Young Folk's Glee Book, 1856; W. B. Bradbury's Metropolitan Glee Book, 1852; Lowell and William Mason's Asoph, 1861; Geo. F. Root's The Coronet, 1865. The plain truth of the matter is that "The Star-Spangled Banner" was slow in gaining popular consideration equal to that accorded to "Hail Columbia" and "America." It took two wars, first the Civil War and, some 30 years later, the Spanish War, to crowd other national songs into the background in favor of "The Star-Spangled Banner," and that fact, it seems to me, is not quite without significance. As last illustration (on Plate XXIII–XXIV) will be found in the Appendix, Firth & Hall's edition of "The Star-Spangled Banner." This edition does not appear to have been copyrighted, and therefore the exact date of publication is unknown to me. The firm of Firth & Hall, so Mr. Warren Pond, of the old and distinguished New York music firm of Wm. A. Pond & Co., informed me on December 18, 1913, "started about the year 1821." Our copyright records show that the *last* copyright entry under Firth & Hall was on September 15, 1845, and the *first* entry under Firth, Hall & Pond on September 24, 1845. It so happens that our copy bears the stamp of "W. E. Millet's Music Saloon, 375 Broadway, N. Y." According to the city directories, Millet was at this address from 1836–37 to 1838–39. From 1839–40 on his address was at 329 Broadway. Obviously, then, the piece must have been published before 1840. The firm of Firth & Hall was not at 1 Franklin Square before 1832. Hence the years 1832 and 1839 give a rough idea of the age of the piece. At any rate, it is the earliest music sheet edition of "The Star-Spangled Banner" in the Library of Congress, though, perhaps, not the earliest published in our country.[a]

Key's poem was accessible to the public as a broadside possibly as early as the morning of September 15, 1814. Here must be quoted what Admiral Preble said on page 725 of the second edition of his "History of our Flag":

> The song on this broadside was enclosed in an elliptical border composed of the common type ornament of the day. Around that border, and a little distance from it, on a line of the same are the words "Bombardment of Fort McHenry." The letters of these words are wide apart, and each one surrounded by a circle of stars. Below the song and within the ellipsis are the words "Written by Francis S. Key, of Georgetown, D. C."

This description applies to the "Fac-simile of broadside as the song first appeared in print," contained in L. H. Dielman's pamphlet "The Seventh Star," published at Baltimore by the board of public works for the Louisiana Purchase Exposition, 1904. However, it may be pointed out by way of correction that merely the initial "F" and not the full name of Francis is printed, that we read M'Henry, not McHenry, that a rather pretty and effective ornamental outer border follows the shape of the broadside, and that the four corners contain additional ornamental designs. What arouses the curiosity

---

[a] This book was in proof sheets when my attention was drawn to an edition of "The Star-Spangled Banner," published by "Geib & Co., No. 23 Maiden Lane," of New York. From the New York city directories I infer that the piece was published between 1816 and 1825. It is facsimiled in Appendix as Plate XXV, by permission of the Boston Public Library.

of the historian most is that Key's authorship is not withheld; that Admiral Preble does not mention this fact at all; that the title of the poem here is "The Star-Spangled Banner," and *that no tune is indicated.*

If Preble's description tallies with a broadside as facsimiled by Dielman, it absolutely differs from "*one of those first printed handbills*" which, so Mrs. Shippen stated in her article, first was in possession of her grandfather, Judge Joseph Hopper Nicholson, then of his wife, after that in Mrs. Shippen's possession, and recently was acquired together with a Star-Spangled Banner autograph by Mr. Henry Walters, of Baltimore. The latter courteously granted permission to examine these treasures, and I found that his broadside (about 6½ by 5½ inches) is without any ornamental design whatsoever, does not mention Key's name at all, and does not bear any title except "Defence of Fort M'Henry." (Facsimile deposited in Library of Congress as Historical Documents, No. 3, by Mr. J. E. H. Post. Compare Appendix, Plate XV.) This is followed by the same historical note as appeared in the Baltimore Patriot of September 20, 1814, then by the indication "Tune: Anacreon in Heaven," and lastly by practically the same text of the poem as it appears in the Judge Nicholson-Widow Nicholson-Mrs. Shippen-Mr. Walters autograph. The only differences, apart from the differences in interpunctuation, etc., are these:

(1) In the first stanza was printed the "Bombs" instead of the bomb.

(2) In the second stanza the misprint "reflected *new* shines" instead of "reflected *now* shines."

(3) In the broadside capital letters frequently appear where they are not found in the autograph, f. i. "The Rocket's," "Land of the Free," "Home of the Brave." On the other hand, the autograph has "Country" whereas this broadside has "country."

Here then are *two* broadsides, both of which are claimed to have belonged to that edition set up on the morning of September 15, 1814. We are not permitted to accept Mrs. Shippen's claims for her broadside offhand, since her account is clearly a mixture of family tradition, personal opinion, and sediment from reading on the subject. The broadsides to be authentic must stand the test of analytical criticism, and if by this process one is eliminated, then all reasonable skepticism will vanish from the other.

The observations called forth by the broadside championed by Preble and Dielman are curious indeed in view of the fact that the Baltimore Patriot, when publishing Key's poem on September 20, 1814, with a prefatory historical note, did not print the title "The Star-Spangled Banner," but instead "Defence of Fort M'Henry," did not mention Key by name at all, but added: "Tune: Anacreon in Heaven." Key's poem—and this is a fact hitherto rarely, if ever, pointed out—made its first appearance in an American songster in the very rare "National Songster, or, a collection of the most admired patriotic songs, on the brilliant victories achieved by the naval and military-heroes . . . First Hagerstown edition," Hagerstown [Md.], John Gruber and Daniel May, *1814* on p. 30–31 under the title of

"DEFENCE OF FORT M'HENRY.

Tune: Anacreon in Heaven.

Wrote by an American Gentleman [!], who was compelled to witness the bombardment of Fort M'Henry, on board of a flag vessel at the mouth of the Patapsco."

Evidently the compiler of the National Songster clipped Key's poem from the Baltimore Patriot or Baltimore American and did not use a copy of this broadside. If, as Mrs. Shippen insists (Pa. Mag. of Hist., 1901–2, pp. 427–428), her grandfather's broadside was "One of those first printed handbills," why was Key's name suppressed in the earliest newspaper accounts after Judge Nicholson had permitted it to go on the handbill which he himself had ordered at a printing office? One might suspect that in view of the vindictive nature of the British it was deemed safer for Mr. Key to suppress the name of the author of "Their foul footsteps' pollution" in a paper of fairly healthy circulation, but this explanation is not plausible, because the historical note in the Baltimore papers could have left no doubt of the offender's identity in the minds of British officers should they have been in a position to catch Key. Possibly Key's modesty would not permit disclosure of his authorship, but what could his modesty avail him if a broadside with his name had already been favorably received by the public of Baltimore? And not merely this, we have the words of Mrs. Shippen:

Judge Nicholson wrote a little piece that appears at the heading of the lines, above which he also wrote the "name of the tune Anacreon in Heaven."

Obviously this action of Judge Nicholson can not apply to that broadside which contains "no little piece" nor indication of the tune, but it does apply to the account in the Baltimore papers. Hence it would have been Judge Nicholson himself who withheld Key's name from the newspapers after he had given it to the public in the Dielman broadside. Furthermore, the Baltimore newspaper account was bodily reprinted in the National Intelligencer September 27, 1814, under the same title "Defence of Fort M'Henry," and at the bottom of the anonymous poem appears the editorial note: "Whoever is the author of those lines they do equal honor to his principles and his talent!" Consequently, not even the editor of a paper printed at Washington, D. C., practically Key's home, knew of his authorship as late as September 27.

Indeed, the anonymous "gentleman" figures in the Baltimore American at least as late as October 19, 1814. There is another suspicious circumstance. It should have aroused surprise before this that Samuel Sands, the apprentice, set up at a moment's notice such an elaborate ornamental handbill as described by Preble and facsimiled by Dielman. The boy must have had remarkably precocious artistic instincts indeed, and very rapid hands and eyes. But why did he refuse to follow copy; why are there several differences between his broadside and the so-called original manuscript? Thus one becomes convinced that *this Dielman broadside is not and can not have been a copy of the one struck off before the publication in the Baltimore Patriot and Baltimore American*, but a copy of a broadside published considerably after that date, when Key's authorship was no longer kept a secret, when his poem had changed—at least in print, the earliest manuscript extant has none—its title from "Defence of Fort M'Henry" to "The Star-Spangled Banner," and when verbal differences in the text had commenced to be quite frequent. The Preble-Dielman broadside thus being eliminated, only the Nicholson-Shippen-Walters broadside remains for serious consideration, and as far as I can see, it contains absolutely nothing to arouse our suspicion. In absence of proof to the contrary, it may indeed be called a copy, perhaps a unique copy, of the original broadside edition!

We turn our attention to the whereabouts of the original manuscript of Key's poem.

Mrs. Shippen writes in the article already quoted:

> Having heard several times of late that there are in existence *several original* copies, of the lines written on the night of September 12 [sic!], 1814 . . , by Francis Scott Key . . . and as I am the fortunate possessor of the only document that could exist of these lines—the *original manuscript*—I will explain how it seems possible that there could be more than one . . . [follows a partly inaccurate account based on Taney] . . . *It is the back of that old letter, unsigned*, that Francis Scott Key (my great-uncle) gave to Judge Joseph Hopper Nicholson (my grandfather) that I possess, together with one of those *first printed* handbills . . . Judge Nicholson [seeing] that the lines given him by Francis Scott Key could be sung to that tune [to Anacreon in Heaven] and in all haste to give the lines as a song to the public, he thus marked it. I possess this rare original manuscript, kept carefully folded by his wife, Rebecca Lloyd Nicholson and taken from her private papers by myself and framed. . . .

This is a clear-cut claim of possession of the *original* manuscript, and yet Mrs. Shippen herself undermines the claim by closing her interesting article thus:

> . . . The first piece of paper on which the lines he composed were written on the night of his arrival in Baltimore I have in my possession; the same that Mr. Key himself gave to Judge Nicholson.

These statements slightly contradict each other, as a careful reading of Chief Justice Taney's account, on which Mrs. Shippen partly (though perhaps indirectly) bases her claim, will prove. According to Taney, Francis Scott Key told him that—

(1) He commenced it [the poem] on the deck of their vessel . . . that he had written *some lines or brief notes* that would aid him in calling them to mind, upon the back of a letter which he happened to have in his pocket; and for some of the lines, as he proceeded, he was obliged to rely altogether on his memory.

(2) He finished it in the boat on his way to the shore.

(3) He *wrote it out as it now stands*, at the hotel, on the night he reached Baltimore and immediately after he arrived.

(4) On the next morning he took it to Judge Nicholson.

Consequently, a distinction is here made between the autograph *sketch* or *draft* of the poem as *commenced* on the cartel vessel and *finished* on the back of a letter in the boat before reaching Baltimore, and the final autograph text as *written out as it now stands* after Key's arrival at Baltimore. It is this first clean copy and final version of the text which Key took to Judge Nicholson for his critical opinion, and, of course, not the first complete sketch or draft on the back of the letter. In the first quotation from her article Mrs. Shippen describes this draft; in the second quotation, the manuscript as written out after Key's arrival at Baltimore. These two manuscripts she confuses, not realizing the bibliographical distinction implied in Chief Justice Taney's narrative. Hence she considered herself Judge Nicholson's heir to the *original* manuscript of "The Star-Spangled Banner," whereas *she really possessed, and Mr. Henry Walters, of Baltimore, now possesses, not the original manuscript* (*i. e.*, the first complete manuscript draft on the back of a letter), *but Key's first clean copy of the original manuscript* (*i. e.*, the manuscript "written out" by Key after his arrival at Baltimore). What became of the real original manuscript we do not know. Presumably Key had no further use for the draft, after he had neatly written out his poem at the hotel and probably destroyed it.

The Library of Congress, by permission of Mr. I. E. H. Post who deposited a photograph facsimile of the Key manuscript as "Historical Documents, No. 1," is now in a position to inclose here for purpose of comparison and analysis a reproduction of this facsimile of the Key manuscript, acquired by Mr. Walters. (Compare Appendix, Plate XVI.) Other facsimiles may be found in the Century Magazine, 1894, page 362, and in Dielman's pamphlet "Maryland, the Seventh Star." Nobody looking at these facsimiles or the original can concede that the latter has the appearance of a sketch or draft. It is too neatly written for that, the lines are too symmetrically spaced and the whole manuscript contains practically only two corrections: In the first stanza Key wrote and then crossed out "*through*" instead of "*by* the dawn's early light," and in the third, "*They have wash'd out*"

instead of "*Their blood has wash'd out.*"   The manuscript contains
no signature, no title, nor indication of tune.   This is mentioned particularly because Mrs. Shippen's article might convey the impression
that the manuscript is "thus marked."   The visible effects of folding
do not point at all to the "old letter" in Key's pocket, since Mrs.
Shippen's manuscript had been "kept carefully folded" by Judge
Nicholson's wife.

Unquestionably, the manuscript now at the Walters Gallery is the
earliest extant of "The Star-Spangled Banner."   It may perhaps
best be described as *the original manuscript of the final and corrected
text.*   In after years Key presented signed autograph copies to friends
and others, but just how many such copies he made is not known.
At any rate, it is not surprising that the existence of several autograph copies led to confusion as to their chronological sequence.   An
attempt shall now be made to separate intelligently such copies as
have come to my notice principally by the way of Admiral Preble's
several contradictory contributions to the subject.

Charles Durang, in the Historical Magazine, 1864, pages 347–348,
claimed that "the original draft, with its interlinations and amendatory erasures, etc., was purchased by the late Gen. George Keim,
of Reading, and I suppose his heirs have it now."

Without the slightest hesitation Preble used this statement in his
book "Our Flag" (1st ed., 1872, p. 495).   In 1874 Preble wrote in
his essay "Three historic flags" (New Engl. Hist. and Gen. Reg.,
pp. 39–40) that this particular copy was

> *Presented* by Mr. Key in 1842 to Gen. George Keim and is now in possession
> of his son Henry May Keim, Esq., of Reading, Penn.   . . .   I have a photo-
> graphic copy of the autograph in the possession of Mr. Keim.

Retracting his former statement about the original draft, with its
erasures, in a footnote on the same page, Preble states that his photograph shows it to be "a fair copy, written out by Mr. Key, and I
learn from Gen. Keim's son that the autograph was presented to his
father by Mr. Key."

A facsimile of this was made for the Baltimore Sanitary Fair in
1864, so Mr. Keim informed Admiral Preble January 8, 1874 (see
New Engl. Hist. and Gen. Reg., 1877, pp. 29), but, if made, it certainly was not included by Kennedy and Bliss in their "Autograph
Leaves," as the Library of Congress copy of this work proves.   Preble gave the text of the Keim copy, though not in facsimile, in his
essay, "Three historic flags" (1874).   In the second edition of his
History of Our Flag (1880) he then informed his readers that Gen.
George Keim's copy had "since [been] presented to the Pennsylvania
Historical Society by his son."   This statement is somewhat puzzling,
because the text of the Keim copy quoted by Preble, 1874, the
dedication "To Gen. Keim," and the undated signature "F. S. Key"

are identical with those of a supposed "Star-Spangled Banner" auto-graph in possession of Mr. Robert A. Dobbin, of Baltimore, Md. When generously loaning this to the Library of Congress for exhibition purposes and granting us the privilege to reproduce it in facsimile (see Appendix, Plate XIX),*Mr. Dobbin, under date of March 24, 1909, wrote:

> Mr. Key was an intimate friend of Gen. Keim of Pennsylvania. On account of this intimacy and as a mark of the friendship which existed between them, Mr. Key gave this copy, which I have loaned you, to General Keim. You will note that Gen. Keim's name is in Mr. Key's handwriting.
>
> Mr. Charles W. Keim, a son of General Keim, came into possession of this copy after the death of his father, and a few years before his own death presented it to my late wife, who was a granddaughter of Mr. Francis Scott Key.

Mr. Dobbin apparently was not aware of the fact that he possessed a photograph, not an original autograph, the photograph even showing the marks of thumb tacks. Consequently, not he but the Pennsylvania Historical Society is in the possession of the Keim copy, which, with its approximate date, 1842, is, of course, as far removed from the original draft with its erasures as is possible. It is here reproduced by permission of the society (see Appendix, Plate XVII.)

Benson John Lossing wrote in footnote (p. 956), in his Pictorial Fieldbook of the War of 1812, first edition, 1868:

> The facsimile of the original manuscript of the first stanza of the "Star-Spangled Banner," given on the opposite page, was first published, by permission of its owner (Mrs. Howard) daughter of the author [Key], in "Autograph Leaves of our Country's Authors," a volume edited by John P. Kennedy and Alexander Bliss for the Baltimore Sanitary Fair, 1864.

Accepting Lossing's statement, Preble in his essay, "Three historic flags," 1874, credited Mrs. Charles Howard, of Baltimore, with the possession of this autograph. As the facsimile in the "Autograph Leaves" shows, it bears the title "The Star-Spangled Banner" and the signature "F. S. Key," but no dedication and no date. The handwriting has not the firmness of youth, and it stands to reason that Key wrote this manuscript in late life. Admiral Preble had occasion in his essay, "The Star-Spangled Banner," New England Historical and Genealogical Register, 1877, pages 28–31, to correct Lossing's statement of ownership, since Mrs. Howard wrote him under date of April 25, 1874:

> I do not think I ever had an autograph of The Star-Spangled Banner. My father [F. S. Key] gave his children from the time they could speak, the habit of committing poetry to memory, and in that way only has the song been preserved to me. Except in one or two words, Mr. Keim's version, as you have it, is the one I have ever remembered.

Though, therefore, Mrs. Howard disclaimed ownership of this particular autograph, yet it must have existed and is, to judge by the facsimile, genuine.

---

*In this edition, Mr. Dobbin's facsimile has been replaced with the Cist autograph.

Another autograph of "The Star-Spangled Banner" was thus described by Preble in his book, Our Flag, 1872:

> A copy of the poem in Key's own handwriting, a copy prepared many years after its composition, and evidently in the *exact* language intended by its author (as it was presented by him to James Mahar, who for thirty years was the gardener of the executive mansion), was a few years since exhibited in the window of Messrs. Phillip & Solomons, on Pennsylvania avenue, Washington. The identity of the handwriting was certified to by Judge Dunlop, Nicholas Callen, Esq., Peter Force, and others, all of whom were intimately acquainted with Mr. Key and perfectly familiar with his style of penmanship. In fact his style was so peculiar and uniform that it would be almost impossible for anyone who had ever noticed it with ordinary care to be mistaken.

This report Preble evidently took from a copy of the National Intelligencer, from which he further quoted "verbatim" the text of the Mahar autograph which evidently bore the title: "The Star-Spangled Banner" and the signature "For Mr. Jas. Mahar, of Washington city, Washington, June 7, 1842. From F. S. Key."

In his essay, "Three historic flags," Preble merely added that the Mahar copy was exhibited at Washington "in 1843, after Mr. Key's death." The present whereabouts of the Mahar copy is unknown to me.

Finally, in his essay, "The Star-Spangled Banner," 1877 (already quoted above), Preble remarked of a copy, dated October 21, 1840:

> It was first published in facsimile in the American Historical and Literary Curiosities (Pl. LV) by John Jay Smith [Sec. Ser. N. Y. 1860, pl. 55] who stated the original was in the possession of Louis J. Cist.

Preble enlivened his narrative by adding a reduced facsimile of this 1840 copy, and he again used it in the second edition of his History of Our Flag, 1880. From there it was reproduced by Miss Mary L. D. Ferris in the New England Magazine, 1890, for her article on "Our national songs" (pp. 483–504). Another facsimile is in the possession of the American Antiquarian Society, Worcester, as Mr. E. M. Barton, the librarian, informed me. The American Antiquarian Society received it on October 21, 1875, from Maj. Albert H. Hoyt, then editor of the New England Historical and Genealogical Register. The original seems to have disappeared until offered for sale as No. 273 in Stan. V. Henkel's catalogue of the Rogers collection of autograph letters, etc., 1895. The added facsimile shows absolute identity in date, signature, orthography, appearance, and every other detail with the facsimile at Worcester.

To sum up, it appears that, not counting the original draft (*i. e.* the real *original* manuscript) at least five copies of "The Star-Spangled Banner" in Francis Scott Key's handwriting exist, or at least existed:

(1) The Judge Nicholson–Mrs. Shippen–Walters copy, 1814. (Walters.)
(2) The Louis J. Cist copy, 1840. (Cist, present whereabouts unknown.)
(3) The supposed Howard copy, ca. 1840. (Howard.)
(4) The Gen. Keim–Pennsylvania Historical Soc. copy. (Pa. Hist. Soc.)
(5) The Mahar copy, 1842. (Mahar.)

There may be other copies, but these five are sufficient for the purpose of showing the changes Francis Scott Key himself made in his poem. The different versions would, as often happens in such cases, be used by different compilers. In course of time verbal inaccuracies would creep from one song book into the other. Also the compilers themselves have sometimes felt justified in improving Key's text. The result of all this has been, of course, that gradually Key's text became unsettled. As early as 1872 Preble marked the verbal differences between certain different versions, and since then surely the confusion has not decreased. Hence, very properly, the cry for an authoritative text has been raised. What should constitute such a text, whether one of Key's own version, or a combination of them, or any later "improved" version, it is not for me to say, though I may be permitted to remark that in my opinion there is no reason for going outside of Key's own intentions. At any rate, I do not consider it my duty to wade through endless song books in order to trace all the verbal inaccuracies and alterations of the text of "The Star-Spangled Banner."[a] The comparison will be extensive enough for all practical purposes if it be limited to Key's own five versions, to the earliest

---

[a] In this connection part of the memorandum of Dr. A. R. Spofford, November 19, 1907, is very instructive. He wrote:

"A collation of this authentic copy [i e., the Cist copy], with several widely circulated collections of songs, shows numerous variations and omissions. Following is a statement of a few of these, with the number of discrepancies found in each:

"Nason (E.). A Monogram [!] on our National Songs. Albany, 1869. (11 variations from original, and one stanza omitted.)

"Higgins (Edwin). The Star-Spangled Banner. Baltimore, 1898. (7 variations.)

"Sousa (J. P.). National and Patriotic Airs of All Lands. Philadelphia, 1890. (14 variations, with a fifth stanza added, which was not written by Key.)

"Bryant (W. C.). Library of Poetry and Song. New York, 1880. (8 variations.)

"Dana (C. D.). Household Poetry. New York, 1859. (7 variations.)

"Coates (H. T.). Fireside Encyclopœdia of Poetry. Philadelphia, 1879. (9 variations.)

"Stedman (E. C.). American Anthology. Boston, 1900. (5 variations.)

"While some of these alterations from the author's manuscript may seem unimportant, others actually change the meaning of the lines, as in the second stanza, where Key wrote—

" 'What is that which the breeze, o'er the towering steep
"As it fitfully blows, half conceals, half discloses?'

"The second line is perverted into—

" 'As it fitfully blows, now conceals, now discloses?'

"In all except three of the reprints before noted this change occurs.

"It is for the worse, for two reasons:

"(1) It destroys the fine image of the wind flapping the flag so as to show and conceal alternately parts of the stars and stripes; while the substitution makes the breeze sometimes conceal the whole star-spangled banner.

"(2) The substitution is bad literary form, since it twice uses the word 'now,' which the author has applied twice in the two lines immediately following."

printed versions, and to the one in his collected poems.   They will be distinguished from each other, where necessary, by the words written in parenthesis.   These printed texts here compared with the earliest manuscript extant are:

(6) The Walters Broadside.   (Broadside I.)
(7) The Preble–Dielman Broadside.   (Broadside II.)
(8) Baltimore Patriot, 1814.   (Patriot.)
(9) Baltimore American, 1814.   (Baltimore Am.)
(10) The "National Songster."   (National Songster.)
(11) Key's Poems, publ. 1857.   (Poems.)

The comparison is based on the Walters text, without esthetic comment.   The (later) title "The Star-Spangled Banner" is taken for granted.   The words that differ are italicized.   Differences in spelling and interpunctuation are disregarded.

O say can [1] *you* see by the dawn's early light
   What so proudly we hail'd [2] *at* the twilight's last gleaming,
Whose [3] *broad stripes & bright stars* through the [4] *perilous* fight
    O'er the ramparts we watch'd, were so gallantly streaming?
      And the rocket's red glare, the [5] *bomb* bursting in air,
      Gave proof through the night that our flag was still there
O say does that star spangled banner yet wave
O'er the land of the free & the home of the brave?

[6] *On the* shore dimly seen through the mists of the deep,
   Where the foe's haughty host in dread silence reposes,
What is that which the breeze, o'er the towering steep,
   As it fitfully blows, [7] *half* conceals, *half* discloses?
      Now it catches the gleam of the morning's first beam
      In full glory reflected now shines [8] *in* the stream
'Tis the star-spangled banner—O long may it wave
O'er the land of the free & the home of the brave!

And where [9] *is that band who* so [10] *vauntingly* swore,
   That the havoc of war & the battle's confusion
A home & a Country should leave us no more?
    [11] *Their* blood has wash'd out [12] *their* foul footstep's pollution
      No refuge could save the hireling & slave
      From the terror of flight or the gloom of the grave,
And the star-spangled banner in triumph doth wave
O'er the land of the free & the home of the brave.

[13] *O* thus be it ever when [14] *freemen* shall stand
   Between their lov'd [15] *home &* [16] *the war's* desolation!
Blest with vict'ry & peace may the heav'n rescued land
   Praise the power that hath made & preserv'd us a nation!
      Then conquer we must, when our cause it is just.
      And this be our motto—"In God is our Trust,"
And the star-spangled banner [17] *in triumph shall* wave
O'er the land of the free & the home of the brave.

DIFFERENCES.

[1] *Ye:* Cist.

[2] *By:* Cist.

[3] *Bright stars & broad stripes:* Cist.

[4] *Clouds of the:* Cist; Pa. Hist. Soc.; Howard; Mahar.

[5] *Bombs:* Broadside I and II; Baltimore Am; Patriot; Poems.

[6] *From:* Broadside II.

[6] *On that:* Cist; Pa. Hist. Soc.; Howard: Poems.

[7] *Now-now:* Poems.

[8] *On:* Cist; Mahar; Patriot.

[9] *Are the foes that:* Pa. Hist. Soc.; Howard.
Are the foes who: Poems.
That host that: Cist.
The foe that: Mahar.

[10] *Sweepingly:* Mahar.

[11] *This:* Mahar.

[12] *His:* Mahar.

[13] *And:* Broadside II.

[14] *Foemen:* Mahar.

[15] *Homes:* Baltimore Am.; Cist; Pa. Hist. Soc.; Howard; Mahar.

[16] *War's:* Mahar.

[17] *O long may it:* Broadside II.

Like other patriotic songs, "The Star-Spangled Banner" has had its share of additional stanzas; that is, of verses suggested by the changing times, the changing spirit of the times, and sectional antagonism. On the other hand, at least one stanza often came to be omitted. It is the third, undoubtedly expressive of bitter sentiment against the English, as was natural and logical in 1814, but rather unnatural and illogical after we were again the friends of England. This apparent defect of Key's text for a national hymn, which should stand above party feeling and chauvinism. led to the composition of one of the two additional stanzas, which shall here be briefly considered. Its origin was narrated to Preble in 1876 by Benjamin Rush in the following words printed by the Admiral in his essay on "The Star-Spangled Banner" (New Eng. Hist. and Gen. Reg., 1877, p. 31):

> The circumstances under which these additional stanzas to the Star-Spangled Banner first came to my hand were briefly adverted to in the Preface to my edition of my father's book, entitled "Recollections of the English and French Courts," published in London in 1871, where I then was. The stanzas were also published; but that need not interfere in the least with your desire to insert them in the second edition of your History of the Flag, wherein I should say they would appropriately come in. The name of the author by whom they were composed was George Spowers, Esq., and this has never been published. I think it eminently due to him now that his name should be given to the public, considering not only the beauty but the admirable sentiments of the stanzas. He had seen in my hands a manuscript copy of the original song, and asked me to lend it to him, which I did. A day or two afterwards he returned it to me with these stanzas. I was quite a boy at the time, at school with my two brothers at Hampstead, near London, while my father was residing in London as minister of the United States. It must have been about the year 1824.

Mr. Spowers's stanza, well-meant but objectionable, because it, too, drags our national hymn into foreign politics, reads:

But hush'd be that strain! They our Foes are no longer;
Lo Britain the right hand of Friendship extends,
And Albion's fair Isle we behold with affection
The land of our Fathers—the land of our Friends!
Long, long may we flourish, Columbia and Britain,
In amity still may your children be found.
And the Star-Spangled Banner and Red Cross together
Wave free and triumphant the wide world around!

The best known of the additional stanzas is the one written by Oliver Wendell Holmes, as he informed Admiral Preble, April 14, 1872, at the request of a lady during our civil war, there being no verse alluding to treasonable attempt against the flag. According to Preble the stanza was first published in the Boston Evening Transcript. Preble received a corrected and amended autograph of the stanza from Holmes, and this he reproduced in facsimile in the second edition of his famous work (p. 730). It reads:

When our land is illumined with liberty's smile,
If a foe from within strikes a blow at her glory,
Down, down with the traitor that dares to defile
The flag of the stars, and the page of her story!
By the millions unchained
Who their birth-right have gained,
We will keep her bright blazon forever unstained;
And the Star-Spangled Banner in triumph shall wave,
While the land of the free is the home of the brave.

It has been noticed before this that not only the text of "The Star-Spangled Banner" but its music is sung and played with noticeable differences. These occur both in the harmonization of the melody and in the melody itself. To trace the discrepancies in the harmonization would hardly be profitable, since the harmonization of any melody will, to a certain degree, always be a matter of individual taste. Often many ways are possible, several equally good—i. e., equally appropriate—and seldom one the only proper one. The harmonization depends, of course, largely on the bass, and since the harmonization of a national song should be simple and easily grasped by the popular mind, there can not be much variance of opinion as to the bass. However, historical considerations will hardly be helpful in this direction. An authoritative harmonization is less a problem of history than of musical grammar, and authoritative it can be only for those who accept the harmonization recommended by a jury of musicians as the authoritative one for the persons under their own musical jurisdiction. It is somewhat different with the melody. True, neither an act of Congress nor the recommendation of a board of musicians will stop the process of polishing and modification (either for better or for worse) which takes place with all folk, traditional, and patriotic songs. Yet it is obviously imperative for musical and other reasons that at least the melody of a national hymn have as much stability and uniformity as can be forced through official channels on the popular mind. The most suitable form of the melody will again be a matter of decision by a jury of musicians, yet it may be interesting and instructive to contrast "To Anacreon in Heaven," as used and modified, partly for verbal reasons, about 1800, with the common versions of its offshoot "The Star-Spangled Banner" of to-day, which from the beginning must have slightly differed from "To Anacreon in Heaven" by dint of the peculiarities of Key's poem. First, the melody as it appears in the Vocal Enchantress, 1783, the earliest version of indisputable date in the Library of Congress, will be compared bar for bar with "Adams and Liberty" in the American Musical Miscellany, 1798 (A. M. M.), and with the version in the Baltimore Musical Miscellany, 1804 (B. M. M.). (The facsimile of the "harmonized" version in Smith's Fifth Book shows it to be too garbled for purposes of melodic comparison. The melody given by Longman & Broderip in the probably earliest publication of the music of "To Anacreon in Heaven" is the same as in the Vocal Enchantress.)

VOCAL ENCHANTRESS, 1783.

DIFFERENCES

Thus the so-called polishing process had begun within one generation after the Sons of Harmony had adopted "To Anacreon in Heaven" as their constitutional song.   How is their club melody sung to the words of "The Star-Spangled Banner" by Americans young and old at the beginning of the twentieth century?   For the purpose of comparison I have selected at random 12 recent songbooks and John Philip Sousa's "National, patriotic, typical airs of all lands" (1890), compiled "by authority" for use in the United States Navy. (Sousa.)   If these few differ so widely in single bars, what discrepancies could be revealed if all the songbooks used in our country were similarly compared?

1. W. H. Aiken.   Part songs for mixed voices for high schools, 1908.
2. C. A. Boyle.   School praise and song, 1903.   (B)
3. C. H. Farnsworth.   Songs for schools, 1906.   (F)
4. A. J. Gantvoort.   School music reader, 1907 (G)
5. B. Jepson's New Standard Music Readers, Seventh year, 1904 (J)
6. McLaughlin-Gilchrist.   Fifth Music Reader, 1906.   (M)
7. Ripley-Tapper.   Harmonic Fifth Reader, 1904.   (R)
8. E. Smith.   Music Course, Book Four, 1908.   (Sm)
9. J. B. Shirley.   Part songs for girl's voices, 1908 (Sh.)
10. H. O. Siefert.   Choice songs, 1902 (Si)
11. C. E. Whiting.   The New public school music course, Third reader, 1909 (W)
12. E. J. A. Zeiner.   The High school song book, 1908.   (Z)

It is not within the province of the Library of Congress to recommend the adoption of one of these different versions against the others, but attention may properly be drawn to "the various efforts made by the music department of the N. E. A. [National Education Association] to secure uniformity in the singing of four of our national songs." A *resumé* of these efforts was recently issued by Mr. A. J. Gantvoort, chairman of the committee in charge of the matter, and reads in part:

> . . . 3. At the N. E. A. meeting, held in Cleveland in July, 1908, Mrs. Frances E. Clark, president of the department, upon motion, appointed A. J. Gantvoort, Elsie M. Shaw, and Osbourne McConathy a committee to make a singable edition of "America," "The Star-Spangled Banner," "Hail Columbia," and the "Red, White and Blue," giving the committee authority to revise words and music for this purpose.
>
> At the meeting in Denver in July, 1909, the chairman reported in open meeting that the committee had been unable to agree and upon motion presented his views by playing the songs on the piano. A motion was then made and carried

a Here we read (p. 791) in the secretary's minutes under date of July 6: "The following arrangements of the melodies of 'America' and of 'The Star-Spangled Banner' were finally agreed upon as the versions which the Department of Music Education recommends as the standard." They follow with the *same incorrect statement of musical authorship* in the heading as in the committee's version of 1912 and it is quite obvious that in 1910 harmony did not reign supreme in the discussions. The principal bar of contention seems to have been the fifth. If, as appears from the quotation below, three versions with different note value for four verses of the same poem were recommended, then it was a foregone conclusion that this recommendation could not be final. Some version would have to be adopted to which all verses could be sung uniformly—a *sine qua non* for mass utterance in national songs.

As reported by the Committee

Verse 1.

What so proud - ly we hailed

As adopted by the Department of Music Education

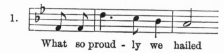

1.

What so proud - ly we hailed

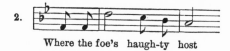

2.

Where the foe's haugh-ty host

4.

Be - tween their loved homes

that the committee be enlarged to seven menbers, but this was reconsidered at an adjourned meeting to allow the number of members to be changed to ten, as follows: A. J. Gantvoort, Elsie M. Shaw, Osbourne McConathy, R. G. Cole, Thomas Tapper, Jessie L. Gaynor, E. B. Birge, Mrs. C. B. Kelsey, Charles H. Farnsworth, and Mrs. Frances E. Clark.

At the meeting held in Boston in 1910, the chairman of the committee made a majority report agreed upon by seven of the members present at a meeting in Cincinnati, and presented copies of its findings before the department. Motion was made and carried to consider only the melodies of these songs, omitting the harmonization. After some discussion, a version of the melody of "America" was unanimously adopted. After considerable discussion, a version of "The Star-Spangled Banner," differing in each stanza, was adopted by a close vote, in which several associate members are said to have voted. The report, as far as was agreed upon, was published in the volume of proceedings in 1910.[a] Upon motion, the committee was continued and ordered to finish its report at the next meeting, which was held in San Francisco in 1911. The chairman of the committee, being absent from this meeting, presented through the president of the department the same report as at the Boston meeting, and after much discussion, upon motion, the action of the Boston meeting was ordered to be reconsidered and the whole matter referred back to the committee for a full report the following year.

At the meeting of 1912 in Chicago, the committee presented a unanimous report, which, after much discussion, was finally unanimously adopted, as presented on the following pages.[b]

A. J. Gantvoort, *Chairman.*

---

[a] See foot note [a], page 100.

[b] Mr. Gantvoort informed me that by an oversight the air there continued to be *incorrectly* attributed to Samuel Arnold. When 1 called his attention to the error, his surprise was comical to behold.

2

THE STAR SPANGLED BANNER

FRANCIS SCOTT KEY, 1779–1843   DR. SAMUEL ARNOLD, 1740–1802

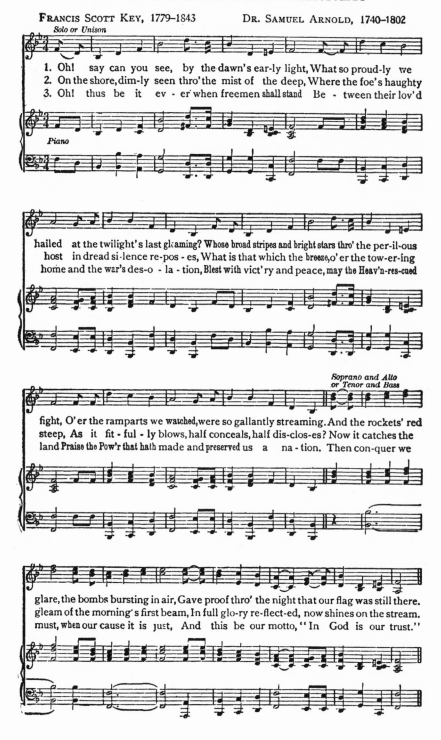

1. Oh! say can you see, by the dawn's ear-ly light, What so proud-ly we
2. On the shore, dim-ly seen thro' the mist of the deep, Where the foe's haughty
3. Oh! thus be it ev - er when freemen shall stand Be - tween their lov'd

hailed at the twilight's last gleaming? Whose broad stripes and bright stars thro' the per-il-ous
host in dread si-lence re-pos - es, What is that which the breeze, o'er the tow-er-ing
home and the war's des-o - la - tion, Blest with vict'ry and peace, may the Heav'n-res-cued

fight, O'er the ramparts we watched, were so gallantly streaming. And the rockets' red
steep, As it fit-ful-ly blows, half conceals, half dis-clos-es? Now it catches the
land Praise the Pow'r that hath made and preserved us a na-tion. Then con-quer we

glare, the bombs bursting in air, Gave proof thro' the night that our flag was still there.
gleam of the morning's first beam, In full glo-ry re-flect-ed, now shines on the stream.
must, when our cause it is just, And this be our motto, "In God is our trust."

THE STAR SPANGLED BANNER. Continued

REFRAIN *Soprano and Alto*

1. Oh!   say   does the   star spang-gled ban-ner   yet

Soprano and Alto

2. 'Tis the star span-gled ban-ner, oh! long may it
3. And the star span-gled ban-ner in tri-umph shall

Bass.

Soprano and Alto

1. Oh!   say   does the   star spang-gled ban-ner   yet
2. Tis the star span-gled. ban-ner, oh! long may it
3. And the star span-gled ban-ner in tri-umph shall

Tenor and Bass

Piano

wave O'er the land of   the   free and the home of the brave?
wave O'er the land of   the   free and the home of the brave?
wave O'er the land of   the   free and the home of the brave!

wave O'er the land of   the   free and the home of the brave?
wave O'er the land of   the   free and the home of the brave!
wave O'er the land of   the   free and the home of the brave!

LITERATURE USED FOR THIS REPORT.

GENERAL.

BANKS, LOUIS ALBERT: Immortal songs of camp and field; the story of their inspiration, together with striking anecdotes connected with their history . . . Cleveland, The Burrows bros. co., 1899 [1898]. 298 p. illus. 8°.

BRINTON, HOWARD FUTHEY: Patriotic songs of the American people. New Haven, The Tuttle, Morehouse & Taylor co., 1900. 111 p. 12°.

BROWN, JAMES DUFF: Characteristic songs and dances of all nations. London, Beyley & Ferguson, c 1901. 276 p. 4°.

BUTTERWORTH, HEZEKIAH: The great composers. Rev. and enl. Boston, Lothrop publishing company, 1894. 5 p. l., 195 p. incl. plates. 18½ cm. pp. 124–160.

CELEBRATED FOLKSONGS AND THEIR TRUE HISTORY. Metronome, 1903, v. 19, no. 9, p. 9.

DANIELL, CARL A.: National airs and who wrote them. Current literature, 1896, vol. 20, pp. 453–454.

ELSON, LOUIS CHARLES: Folk songs of many nations, collected and ed., with preface and annotations. Cincinnati, Chicago [etc.] The J. Church company [1905]. 1 p. l., 171 p. 28 cm.

ELSON, LOUIS CHARLES: The national music of America and its sources. Boston, L. C. Page and company, 1900 [1899]. vi, v–viii, 9–326 p. 4 port. (incl. front.). 17½ cm. (See also his Hist, of Am. Music, 1904, pp. 140–164.)

FERRIS, MARY L. D.: Our national songs [illus. fac-similes, especially of letter by Rev. S. F. Smith, dated 1889 and narrating origin of "America"]. New England magazine, 1890. new ser. vol. 2, pp. 483–504.

FITZ-GERALD, S. J. ADAIR: Stories of famous songs. London, 1898.

JOHNSON, HELEN (KENDRICK) "Mrs. Rossiter Johnson:" Our familiar songs and those who made them. More than three hundred standard songs of the English-speaking race, arranged with piano accompaniment, and preceded by sketches of the writers and histories of the songs. New York, H. Holt and co. 1881. xiii, 660 p. 4°.

JOHNSON, HELEN (KENDRICK) "Mrs. Rossiter Johnson:" Our familiar songs and those who made them; three hundred standard songs of the English speaking race, arranged with piano accompaniment, and preceded by sketches of the writers and histories of the songs. New York, H. Holt and company, 1889. xiii, 660 p. 25½ cm.

JOHNSON, HELEN KENDRICK AND DEAN, FREDERIC: Famous songs and those who made them . . . New York, Bryan, Taylor & co. 1895. 2 v. 4°. [The American national songs here treated are contained in the first volume.]

KOBBÉ, GUSTAV.: Famous American songs. New York, T. Y. Crowell & co. [1906]. xvii, [1], 168, [1] p. incl. front. plates, ports., facsims. 20½ cm.

McCARTY, WILLIAM: Songs, odes, and other poems on national subjects. Philadelphia, 1842. 3v.

MEAD, LEON: The songs of freedom [includes M. Keller's "The American hymn" with music]. Chautauquan, 1900, vol. 31, pp. 574–584.

MOORE, FRANK: Songs and ballads of the American Revolution. New York. D. Appleton & co., 1856.

NASON, ELIAS: A monogram on our national song. Albany, J. Munsell, 1869. 69 p. 8°.

NATIONAL MELODIES OF AMERICA: The poetry by George P. Morris, esq., adapted and arranged by Chas. E. Horn. Part I. New York, 1839. [Review of the collection which does not deal with *national* melodies but rather with *folk* melodies with a leaning towards negro songs.] Southern literary messenger, 1839. vol. 5, pp. 770–773.

NATIONAL SONGS [merely reprint of two prize poems "Sons of America" and "Old Glory"]. Iowa historical record, 1895, vol. 11, pp. 329–331.

OUR NATIONAL SONGS; with numerous original illustrations by G. T. Tobin. New York, F. A. Stokes co. [1898]. 128 p. illust. 24° [words only.]

PREBLE, HENRY GEORGE: History of the flag of the United States of America. Second revised edition. Boston, A. Williams and co. 1880. 3 p. 715–768. [Chapter on "National and patriotic songs," also first edition, 1872, used.]

REDDALL, HENRY FREDERIC: Songs that never die . . . enriched with valuable historical and biographical sketches . . . Philadelphia National Publishing co. [c1892]. 615 p. 8°.

RIMBAULT, EDWARD F.: American national songs [with music]. Leisure hour, 1876, vol. 25, pp. 90–92.

SAFFELL, W. T. R.: Hail Columbia, the Flag and Yankee Doodle Dandy. Baltimore, T. Newton Kurtz, 1864. 123 p. 8°.

SMITH, NICHOLAS: Stories of great national songs. Milwaukee, The Young churchman co. [etc. etc., 1899]. 238 p. 2 pl., 18 port. (incl. front.). 19½ cm.

SONNECK, O. G.: Bibliography of early secular American music. Washington, D. C. Printed for the author by H. L. McQueen, 1905. x, 194 p. 29 cm.

SONNECK, O. G.: Report on "The Star-Spangled Banner," "Hail Columbia," "America," "Yankee Doodle." Washington, Govt. print. off., 1909. 255 p. incl. 21 double facsim. 26½ cm.

SPOFFORD, AINSWORTH R.: The lyric element in American history. Columbia Historical Society, Records, 1904, vol. 7. (Same printed separately.)

SOUSA, JOHN PHILIP: National, patriotic, and typical airs of all lands, with copious notes. Philadelphia, H. Coleman [c1890]. 283 p. 4°. [Compiled by authority of the Secretary of the Navy, 1889, for the use of the department.]

STEVENSON, E. IRENAEUS: Our "national" songs. Independent, 1897, vol. 49, nos. 2526–2561.

WAYNE, FLYNN: Our national songs and their writers. National magazine, 1899/1900, vol. 11, pp. 284–296.

WHITE, RICHARD GRANT: National hymns. How they are written and how they are not written. A lyric and national study for the times. New York, Rudd & Carleton [etc.], 1861. x, [11]–152 p. incl. front. 23 cm.

STAR SPANGLED BANNER—SPECIAL

ANTIQUARY: Origin of "The Star spangled banner." Music, 1891–92, vol. 1, pp. 469–471.

APPLETON, NATHAN: The Star Spangled Banner. An address delivered at the Old South Meeting House, Boston . . . on June 14, 1877. Boston, Lockwood, Brooks & Co., 1877. 8°. 34p. [on the history of the flag, the song, etc.]

BARTLETT, HOMER N.: E pluribus unum. Musical courier, 1912, v. 64, no. 23, p. 37.

BLAKE, JOHN HENRY: American national anthem. "Star spangled banner" made "singable" for the voices of the people. History of the origin of the words and music . . . New York, J. H. Blake, 1912. 3 p. l., 10 p. 34 cm.

BROWNE, C. A.: The story of "The Star-Spangled Banner." Musician, 1907, v. 12, p. 541.

CARPENTER, JOHN C.: "The Star Spangled Banner" [with port. and facsimile]. Century magazine, 1894, vol. 48, pp. 358–363.

CHAPPELL, WM.: "The Star-Spangled Banner" and "To Anacreon in Heaven" [on the authorship of John Stafford Smith]. Notes and Queries (London), 1873, 4th ser., vol. 11, pp. 50–51.

CUMMINGS, WILLIAM H.: English music (1604 to 1904), being the lectures given at the Music Loan Exhibition . . . 1904, London, The Walter Scott Publishing Co., 1906. (On pp. 51–52 his comment on "To Anacreon in Heaven.")

DORSEY, MRS. ANNA H. Origin of the Star Spangled Banner [reprinted from Washington *Sunday Morning Chronicle*]. (Dawson's) Historical magazine, 1861, vol. 5, pp. 282–283.

FLOOD, W. H. GRATTAN: The original air of "The Star Spangled Banner." Church music, 1909, v. 4, pp. 281–282.

FLOOD, W. H. GRATTAN: The Irish origin of the tune of The Star Spangled Banner. Ave Maria, July 6, 1912, pp. 19–20.

FOR A NEW NATIONAL HYMN. North American review, 1906, vol. 183, pp. 947–948.

THE FRANCIS SCOTT KEY MEMORIAL. Munsey's magazine, 1898, vol. 20, pp. 325–326.

GEBHART, D. R.: The national anthem. School music, 1911, v. 12, no. 57, pp. 16–17, 20.

HAGNER, A. B.: Genesis of The Star Spangled Banner. The Historical Bulletin (Washington, D. C.), 1905, v. 6, no. 2, pp. 29–33 (with facsimile of the "author's first draft").

HENRY, REV. H. T.: The air of "The Star-Spangled Banner." Records of the American Catholic Hist. Soc., 1913, v. 24, no. 4, pp. 289–335.

HIGGINS, EDWIN: The national anthem "The Star Spangled Banner," Francis Scott Key, and patriotic lines. Baltimore, 1898 [illustrated reprint of the poem with a brief biographical sketch, 12 p. 16°].

HILL, MARION: The Star Spangled Banner. Does it get weighed? Or yet wade? Uncertainty of many school children on the subject. McClure's magazine, 1900, vol. 15, pp. 262–267 [not historical].

KEY, FRANCIS SCOTT: Poems . . . with an introductory letter by Chief Justice Taney. New York, R. Carter & Bros., 1857 [the letter narrates "the incidents connected with the origin of the song The Star Spangled Banner" as told the author by Key].

K[IDSON], FRANK: Star Spangled Banner. Grove's dictionary of music and musicians, 2d ed., 1908. vol. 4, pp. 674–675.

KING, HORATIO: The Star Spangled Banner. Magazine of American history, 1883. Vol. X, pp. 516–517.

KINNEAR, WM. B.: The Star Spangled Banner melody. School music, 1912, v. 13, no. 58, pp. 11–15.

LOSSING, BENSON JOHN: The pictorial field-book of the war of 1812. Facsimile of the original manuscript of the first stanza of "The Star Spangled Banner," reprinted from Kennedy and Bliss' "Autograph leaves of our country authors;" origin of the hymn narrated in footnote to pp. 956–958.

LEINARD, L.: Story of our National song. Piano magazine, 1910, v. 3, no. 6, pp. 31–36.

McLAUGHLIN, J. FAIRFAX: "The Star-Spangled Banner!" who composed the music for it. It is American, not English. American Art Journal, 1896. vol. 68, No. 13, pp. 194–195.

MEAD, LUCIA AMES: Our National Anthem [against "The Star Spangled Banner"]. Outlook, 1903. vol. 75, p. 616.

MARYLAND, BOARD OF PUBLIC WORKS: The seventh star. Facts and figures about the State of Maryland. Her past greatness and her present prosperity . . . Pub. by the board of public works for the Louisiana purchase exposition. Maryland day, September 12th, 1904. Baltimore, Md. Press of Lucas brothers [1904] [22] p. front., illus., ports., facsims. 23½ cm. Contains facsimiles. Compiled by [L. H. Dielman].

A MONUMENT TO FRANCIS SCOTT KEY [by Doyle and port. of K. on p. 128]. The Critic, 1898. new ser. vol. 30, p. 129.

MUNICIPAL BANDS and our National air. American musician, 1912, v. 28, no. 16, pp. 10–11.

THE NATIONAL ANTHEM [on the official adoption of "The Star Spangled Banner" by the Army and Navy]. Outlook, 1903. vol. 75, p. 245.

NATIONAL HYMNOLOGY [on our national anthem with special reference to "The Star Spangled Banner"]. Scribner's magazine, 1907. vol. 42, pp. 380–381.

PINKERTON, WILLIAM: The Star Spangled Banner. Notes & Queries, 1864. 3d ser. vol. 6, pp. 429–430.

PREBLE, GEORGE HENRY: The Star Spangled Banner, autographic copies, additional verses, etc. (8°. 7p.) published separately in ed. of 100 copies with facsimile. Boston, 1876.

PREBLE, GEO. HENRY: The Star Spangled Banner. Autograph copies, additional verses, etc. Communicated by Rear Admiral . . . [with facsimile of copy dated Oct. 21, 1840]. New England Historical and Genealogical register, 1877. vol. 31, pp. 28–31.

PREBLE, GEO. HENRY: Three historic flags and three September victories [contains important matter on "The Star Spangled Banner" especially the different autographs]. New England Historical and Genealogical Register, 1874. vol. 28, pp. 17–41.

ROSEWIG, A. H.: "Anacreon in Heaven," the origin of "The Star Spangled Banner" with its complete history. Philadelphia c1909. 4 p. fol.

SALISBURY, STEPHEN: The Star Spangled Banner and national songs [Read at a meeting of the American Antiquarian Society, in Worcester, Oct. 21]. Dwight's journal of music, 1872. vol. 32, pp. 332–333.

SALISBURY, STEPHEN: The Star Spangled Banner and national airs. [Read before the American Antiquarian Society, Oct. 21, 1872.] American Historical Record, 1872. vol. 1, pp. 550–554.

SALISBURY, STEPHEN: An essay on the Star Spangled Banner and national songs. Read before the society, October 21, 1872. Worcester, 1873. 8°. 15 p. Reprinted from the Proceedings of the American Antiquarian Society.

—— Same [second ed.] with additional notes and songs. Worcester, 1873. 8°. 24 p. (ed. of 100.)

SALISBURY, STEPHEN: The Star Spangled Banner and national songs. American Antiquarian Society, Proceedings, 1873, pp. 43–53.

SCHELL, FRANK H: Our great national hymn "The Star Spangled Banner" and its origin [inconsequential note]. Leslie's weekly, 1898. vol. 87, p. 85.

[THE SELECTION OF THE MUSIC FOR THE "STAR SPANGLED BANNER" by Ferdinand Durang.] Iowa Historical Record, 1897. vol. 13, p. 144.

SHIPPEN, REBECCA LLOYD: The original manuscript of "The Star Spangled Banner." Pennsylvania Magazine of Hist. & Biogr., 1901. vol. 25, pp. 427–428.

SMITH, F. S. KEY: Fort McHenry and the "Star Spangled Banner" [with port. of Francis Scott Key]. The Republic magazine, 1908. vol. 1, No. 4, pp. 10–20.

SMITH, FRANCIS SCOTT KEY: Francis Scott Key, author of the Star Spangled Banner; what else he was and who. Washington, D. C., Key-Smith and Co., [c1911]. 104 p. 4 pl., 3 port. (incl. front.) facsim. 19½cm.

THE STAR SPANGLED BANNER [facsimile of the handwriting of the author, Francis S. Key, dated Washington, October 21, 1840, formerly in possession of Lewis J. Cist]. Smith's American historical and literary curiosities, 2d ser. Philadelphia, Pl. LV.

THE STAR SPANGLED BANNER: Dwight's journal of music, 1861. vol. 19, pp. 37, 39, 46.

THE STAR SPANGLED BANNER: American Historical Record, 1873. vol. 2, pp. 24–25.

STAR SPANGLED BANNER [inconsequential note]. American notes and queries, 1888. vol. 1, pp. 199.

THE STAR SPANGLED BANNER [criticism of J. H. Blake's pamphlet]. Musical news, 1912. vol. 42, p. 225.

STAR SPANGLED BANNER in choral form. School music monthly, 1912. vol. 13, no. 61.

THE STAR SPANGLED BANNER. [Facsimile of four stanzas in autograph of F. S. Key, dated Oct. 21, 1840] Henkel's Catalogue of autograph letters, etc. No. 738, p. 50.

[TANEY, ROGER B.]: "The Star Spangled Banner" [extract from a letter dated 1856, written to her giving the origin of the words and] Contributed by Mrs. Rebecca Lloyd Shippen. Pennsylvania magazine of history and biography, 1898/99. vol. 22, pp. 321–325.

UNEDA. Note on "The Star Spangled Banner." Notes and Queries (London), 2d ser., 1861. vol. 12, p. 310.

WARNER, JOHN L.: The origin of the American National anthem called the Star Spangled Banner. [Read before the Pennsylvania Historical Society, at its meeting, 1867]. (Dawson's) Historical magazine, 1867. vol. 11, pp. 279–280.

WILCOX, MARION: America's National song [The Star Spangled Banner] Harper's weekly, 1905. vol. 49, p. 373.

X. The Star Spangled Banner . . . Musical times, 1896. vol. 37, pp. 516–519.

INDEX

ILLUSTRATIONS

PLATE I.

Star Spangled Banner.

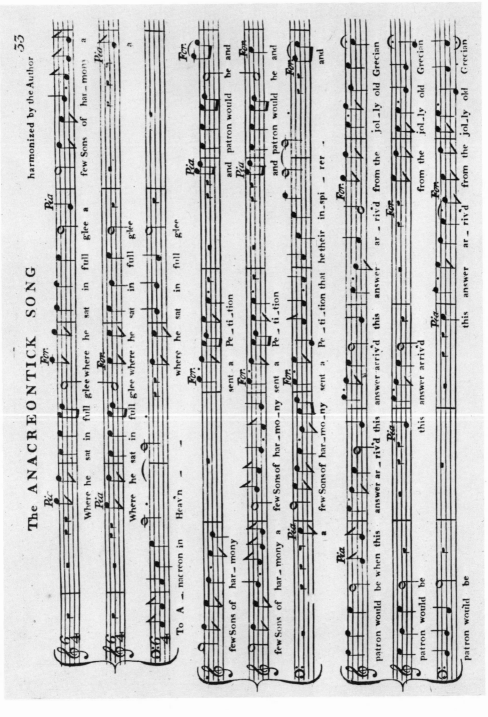

FROM JOHN STAFFORD SMITH'S "FIFTH BOOK OF CANZONETS," LONDON [1799].

TITLE-PAGE OF JOHN STAFFORD SMITH'S "FIFTH BOOK OF CANZONETS," LONDON [1799].

THE ANACREONTIC SONG

As Sung at the Crown and Anchor Tavern in the Strand, LONDON, With General Admiration.

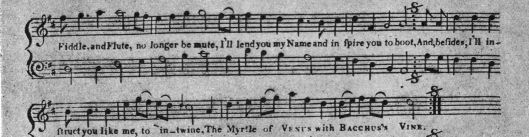

To ANACREON in Heav'n, where he sat in full Glee, A few Sons of Harmony sent a Petition, That He their In-spirer and Patron would be; when this Answer ar-riv'd from the JOLLY OLD GRECIAN "Voice, Fiddle, and Flute, no longer be mute, I'll lend you my Name and inspire you to boot, And, besides, I'll in-struct you like me, to in-twine, The Myrtle of VENUS with BACCHUS'S VINE.

2

The News through OLYMPUS immediately flew;
When OLD THUNDER pretended to give himself Airs.
If these Mortals are suffer'd their Scheme to persue,
The Devil a Goddess will stay above Stairs.
   Hark! already they cry,
   In Transports of Joy,
Away to the Sons of ANACREON we'll fly,
And there, with good Fellows, we'll learn to intwine
The Myrtle of VENUS with BACCHUS'S VINE.

3

The YELLOW-HAIR'D GOD & his nine lusty Maids,
From HELICON'S Banks will incontinent flee,
IDALIA will boast but of tenantless Shades,
And the bi-forked Hill a mere Desart will be
   My Thunder, no fear on't,
   Shall soon do it's Errand,
And, Dam'me! I'll swinge the Ringleaders I warrant,
I'll trim the young Dogs, for thus daring to twine
The Myrtle of VENUS with BACCHUS'S VINE.

4

APOLLO rose up; and said, Pr'ythee ne'er Quarrel,
Good KING of the GODS, with my Vot'ries below;
Your Thunder is useless — then, shewing his Laurel,
Cry'd. "Sic evitabile Fulmen, you know!
   Then over each Head
   My Laurels I'll spread;
So my Sons from your Crackers no Mischief shall dread,
Whilst snug in their Club-room, they Jovially twine
The Myrtle of VENUS with BACCHUS'S VINE.

5

Next MOMUS got up, with his risible Phiz,
And Swore with APOLLO he'd chearfully join
The full Tide of Harmony still shall be his,
But the SONG, and the CATCH, and the LAUGH shall be mine,
   Then, JOVE, be not jealous
   Of these honest Fellows.
Cry'd JOVE, We relent, since the truth you now tell us
And swear, by OLD STYX, that they long shall intwine
The Myrtle of VENUS with BACCHUS'S VINE.

6

Ye Sons of ANACREON, then, join Hand in hand;
Preserve Unanimity, Friendship, and Love!
'Tis your's to support what's so happily Plann'd;
You've the Sanction of GODS, and the FIAT of JOVE.
   While thus we agree
   Our Toast let it be.
May our Club flourish happy, united, and free!
And long may the Sons of ANACREON intwine
The Myrtle of VENUS with BACCHUS'S VINE.

Publish'd by ANNE LEE in Dame Street (N.º 2.)

The ANACREONTIC Song

Sung by **Mr. Incledon** with great Applause.

DUBLIN. Publifhed by **E. RHAMES**, at her MUSICAL CIRCULATING LIBRARY, N⁰16, Exchange Street

VIVACE. To ANACREON in Heav'n, where he fat in full Glee, a few Sons of Harmony fent a Petition, that

he their infpirer and Patron wou'd be; when this Anfwer arriv'd from the Jolly old GRECIAN, "Voice

Fiddle and Flute, no longer be mute, I'll lend you my Name, and infpire you to boot: and be—

—fides I'll inftruct you, like me, to intwine the MYRTLE of VENUS with BACCHUS'S VINE."

2
The news through OLYMPUS immediately flew,
When OLD THUNDER pretended to give himfelf airs:
If thefe Mortals are fuffer'd their fcheme to purfue,
The Devil a GODDESS will ftay above ftairs.
Hark! already they cry
In tranfports of joy,
Away to the Sons of ANACREON we'll fly,
And there, with good fellows, we'll learn to intwine
The MYRTLE of VENUS with BACCHUS'S VINE.

3
The YELLOW HAIR'D GOD and his NINE fufty MAIDS
From HELICON's Banks will incontinent flee;
IDALIA will boaft but of tenantlefs Shades,
And the BIFORKED HILL a mere Defert will be.
My Thunder, no fear on't,
Shall foon do its errand,
And foundly I'll fwinge the Ringleaders I warrant:
I'll trim the young Dogs, for thus daring to twine
The MYRTLE of VENUS with BACCHUS'S VINE.

Ye Sons of ANACREON, then, join hand in hand,
Preferve Unanimity, Friendfhip and Love;
'Tis yours to fupport what's fo happily plann'd
You've the Sanction of GODS, and the FIAT of JOVE.

4
APOLLO rofe up, and faid, Prythee ne'er quarrel
Good KING of the GODS, with my Vot'ries below;
Your Thunder is ufelefs — then fhewing his Laurel
Cried, Sic evitabile Fulmen, you know.
Then over each head
My Laurels I'll fpread,
So my Sons from your Crackers no mifchief fhall dread,
Whilft fnug in their Club-room, they jovially twine
The MYRTLE of VENUS with BACCHUS'S VINE.

5
Next MOMUS got up, with his rifible Phiz,
And fwore with APOLLO he'd chearfully join.
The full tide of harmony ftill fhall be his,
But the SONG, and the CATCH, and the LAUGH fhall be mine.
Then JOVE be not jealous
Of thefe honeft fellows.
Cried JOVE, We relent, fince the truth you now tell us:
And fwear by OLD STYX that they long fhall intwine
The MYRTLE of VENUS with BACCHUS'S VINE.

6
While thus we agree, — Our Toaft let it be
May our Club flourifh, happy, united and free!
And long may the SONS of ANACREON intwine
The MYRTLE of VENUS with BACCHUS'S VINE.

FOR THE GUITAR.

VOCAL MAGAZINE. 147

Be thou but mine, with rofy health,
Let dear content be by;
The reft I'll leave the fons of wealth,
Without a fingle figh.

RECITATIVE.

Thus fang the youth, whofe breaft was ho-
nour's throne,
Whofe mind fimplicity had made her own;
Till, far afield, the tinkling village bells
Call'd fportive echo from her grots and cells.
They left the grove, unto the dance they fped;
Revel'd till eve, and the next morn were wed.

AIR.

Now love and fond wifhes concur
To make them the talk of the plain;
The maids take example from her,
And the fhepherds all copy the fwain.

Where e'er fuch examples are fhown,
Who of wedlock can ever repent;
Where conftancy governs the throne,
The fubjects are fure of content.

RECITATIVE.

To feek no more, let lovers learn from hence,
Till hymen wills, than Love and Innocence.

SONG 564.

LOVE, thou'rt the beft of human joys,
Our chiefeft happinefs below!
All other pleafures are but toys;
Mufic without thee is but noife,
Beauty but an empty fhow.

Heav'n, that knew beft what man cou'd move,
And raife his thoughts above the brute;
Said, Let him be, and let him love.
That only muft his foul improve,
Howe'er philofophers difpute.

SONG 565.

INVOCATION TO HEALTH.

SWEETEST health, of rofy hue,
Brighteft daughter of the fky,
Hafte, and bid thofe fkies adieu,
And to Cornelia's bofom fly!
Hafte thee, nymph, ah! hafte along,
Come and liften to my fong:
'Tis for you I tune my lay;
Faireft virgin, hafte away.

Wherefore, goddefs, haft thou fled,
Whence fo fweetly thou didft reft;
In fo calm, fo foft a bed,
With content, thy fifter, bleft.
Come, ah! come, and with thee bring
Drops from Lethe's foothing fpring;
Balm from Tempe's fragrant vales,
Nectar which the gods regales.

Goddefs come! and on her breaft
Shed thy healing influence;

Let no cares that fpot moleft,
Drive all pain and forrow thence.
Why delay'ft thou, goddefs, fay?
Virtue calls thee, come away;
Fly'ft thou from that heav'nly cell,
Where virtue's felf delights to dwell?

Hafte thee, faireft, pr'ythee hafte,
Nor to quit one heaven fear;
Hie thee to Cornelia's breaft,
Thou wilt make a heaven there.

SONG 566.

ANACREONTIC SOCIETY.

Written by RALPH TOMLINSON, Efq.

TO Anacreon, in Heav'n, where he fat in
full glee;
A few fons of harmony fent a petition,
That he their infpirer and patron would be;
When this anfwer arriv'd from the jolly old
Grecian—
Voice, fiddle, and flute,
No longer be mute;
I'll lend ye my name, and infpire ye to boot:
And, befides, I'll inftruct ye, like me, to intwine
The myrtle of Venus with Bacchus's vine.

The news through Olympus immediately flew;
When old Thunder pretended to give him-
felf airs—
If thefe mortals are fuffer'd their fcheme to
purfue,
The devil a goddefs will ftay above ftairs.
Hark! already they cry,
In tranfports of joy,
A fig for Parnaffus! to Rowley's we'll fly;
And there, my good fellows, we'll learn to
intwine
The myrtle of Venus with Bacchus's vine.

The yellow-hair'd god, and his nine fufty
maids,
To the hill of old Lud will incontinent flee,
Idalia will boaft but of tenantlefs fhades,
And the biforked hill a mere defart will be.
My thunder, no fear on't,
Will foon do it's errand,
And, dam'me! I'll fwinge the ringleaders,
I warrant.
I'll trim the young dogs, for thus daring to twine
The myrtle of Venus with Bacchus's vine.

Apollo rofe up; and faid, Pr'ythee ne'er quarrel,
Good king of the gods, with my vot'ries
below:
Your thunder is ufelefs—then, fhewing his
laurel,
Cry'd, *Sic evitabile fulmen*, you know!
Then over each head
My laurels I'll fpread;
So my fons from your crackers no mifchief
fhall dread,
Whilft fnug in their club-room, they jovially
twine
The myrtle of Venus with Bacchus's vine.
T 2

[336]

SONG CLXVII.

To Anacreon, in heav'n, where he fat in full glee,

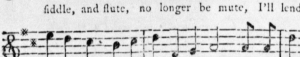

a few fons of harmony fent a pe - ti - tion, that he

their in-fpir-er and patron would be ; when this

anfwer ar-riv'd from the jol-ly old Grecian—" Voice,

fiddle, and flute, no longer be mute, I'll lend

you my name and infpire you to boot ; and, befides,

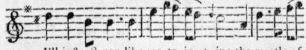

I'll inftruct you like me to in - twine the myrtle of
Venus

PLATE VI.

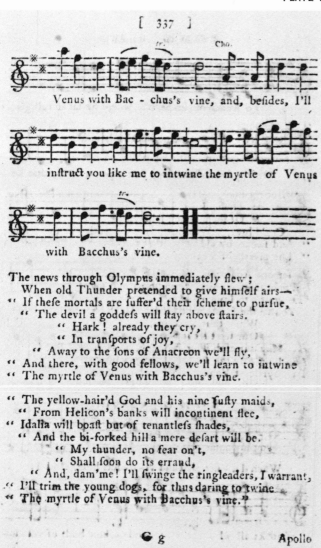

[337]

Venus with Bac - chus's vine, and, befides, I'll instruct you like me to intwine the myrtle of Venus with Bacchus's vine.

The news through Olympus immediately flew;
　When old Thunder pretended to give himfelf airs—
" If thefe mortals are fuffer'd their fcheme to purfue,
　" The devil a goddefs will ftay above ftairs.
　　　" Hark! already they cry,
　　　" In tranfports of joy,
　　" Away to the fons of Anacreon we'll fly,
" And there, with good fellows, we'll learn to intwine
" The myrtle of Venus with Bacchus's vine.

" The yellow-hair'd God and his nine fufty maids,
　" From Helicon's banks will incontinent flee,
" Idalia will boaft but of tenantlefs fhades,
　" And the bi-forked hill a mere defart will be.
　　　" My thunder, no fear on't,
　　　" Shall foon do its errand,
　" And, dam'me! I'll fwinge the ringleaders, I warrant,
" I'll trim the young dogs, for thus daring to twine
" The myrtle of Venus with Bacchus's vine."

G g　　　　　　　　　Apollo

"TO ANACREON IN HEAVEN," FROM "THE VOCAL ENCHANTRESS,"
LONDON, 1783.

THE ANACREONTIC SONG

Sung by Mr. INCLEDON with universal Applause.

To A-na-creon in Heav'n where he sat in full Glee, A few Sons of Harmony sent a petition, That he their in-

spirer and Patron wou'd be; when this Answer ar—riv'd from the Jolly Old Grecian: Voice, Fiddle, and Flute, no

longer be mute, I'll lend you my Name and in-spire you to boot, And, be—sides, I'll instruct you like me, to intwine, The

Myrtle of Venus with Bacchus's Vine.

II.
The News through Olympus immediately flew;
When old Thunder pretended to give himself Airs,
If these Mortals are suffer'd their Scheme to pursue,
The Devil a Goddess will stay above Stairs.
Hark! already they cry,
In Transports of Joy,
Away to the Sons of Anacreon we'll fly,
And there, with good Fellows, we'll learn to intwine
The Myrtle of Venus with Bacchus's Vine.

III.
The Yellow Hair'd God and his nine fusty Maids,
From Helicon's Banks will incontinent flee,
Idalia will boast but of tenantless Shades,
And the big forked Hill a mere Desart will be,
My Thunder, no fear on't
Shall soon do its Errand,
And, Dam' me, I'll swinge the Ringleaders I warrant,
I'll trim the young Dogs, for thus daring to twine
The Myrtle of Venus with Bacchus's Vine.

"TO ANACREON IN HEAVEN," FROM EXSHAW'S LONDON MAGAZINE, DUBLIN, 1791.

PLATE VIII.

THE ORIGINAL LONGMAN & BRODERIP, 26 CHEAPSIDE ISSUE OF
"THE ANACREONTIC SONG" [178–].

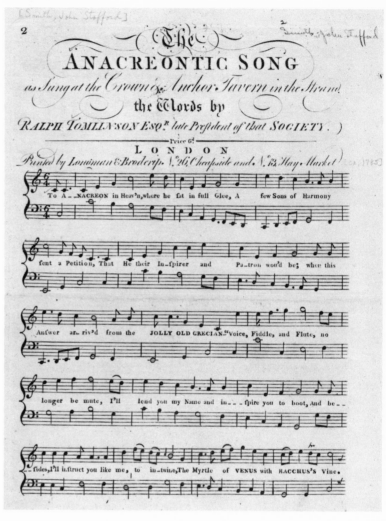

PLATE IX.

Star Spangled Banner.

PLATE X.

26

Hard, hard is my fate! oh, how galling my chain
    My life's steer'd by misery's chart—
And 'tho 'gainst my tyrants I scorn to complain,
    Tears gush forth to ease my sad heart :
I disdain e'en to shrink, tho' I feel the sharp lash;
    Yet my breast bleeds for her I adore :
While round me the unfeeling billows will dash,
    I sigh!—and still tug at the oar.

How fortune deceives!—I had pleasure in tow,
    The port where she dwelt we'd in view;
But the wish'd nuptial morn was o'erclouded with
    And, dear Anne, I hurried from you.   [woe,
Our shallop was boarded, and I borne away,
    To behold my lov'd Anne no more!
But dispair wastes my spirits, my form feels decay-
    He sigh'd—and expir'd at the oar!

· · · · · ·

ANACREON IN HEAVEN.

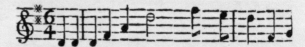

To Anacreon in Heav'n where he sat in ful

glee, A few sons of harmony sent a petition

PLATE XI.

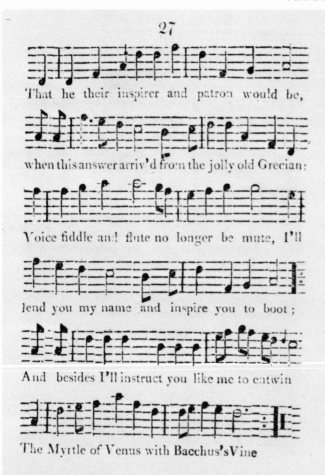

27

That he their inspirer and patron would be,

when this answer arriv'd from the jolly old Grecian:

Voice fiddle and flute no longer be mute, I'll

lend you my name and inspire you to boot;

And besides I'll instruct you like me to entwin

The Myrtle of Venus with Bacchus's Vine

The news through Olympus immediately flew,
When old Thunder pretented to give himself
airs:

FROM "BALTIMORE MUSICAL MISCELLANY," 1804.

Star Spangled Banner.

PLATE XII.

2

In a cline, whofe rich vales feed ȳ marts of the world,
Whofe fhores are unfhaken by Europe's commotion,
The Trident of Commerce fhould never be hurl'd,
To incenfe the legitimate powers of the ocean ;
But fhould Pirates invade,
Though in thunder array'd,
Let your Cannon declare the free Charter of Trade ;
For ne'er fhall the fons of COLUMBIA be flaves,
While the earth bears a plant or the fea rolls its waves

3

The fame of our arms, of our laws the mild fway,
Had juftly enobled our nation in ftory,
Till the dark clouds of Faction obfcur'd our young day,
And invelop'd the fun of American glory ;
But let Traitors be told,
Who their Country have fold,
And barter'd their God for his image in gold
That ne'er will the fons &c.

4

While France her huge limbs bathes recumbent in blood
And fociety's bafe threats with wide diffolution,
May peace like the Dove, who return'd from the flood,
Find an Ark of abode in our mild CONSTITUTION,
But though peace is our Aim,
Yet the boon we difclaim,
If bought with our SOV'REIGNTY, JUSTICE or FAME,
For ne'er will the fons &c.

5

Tis the fire of the flint each American warms,
Let Rome's haughty Victors beware of collifion,
Let them bring all the Vaffals of Europe in arms,
We're a World by ourfelves & difdain a divifion ;
While with patriot pride,
To our laws we're allied,
No foe can fubdue us no faction divide,
For ne'er fhall the fons &c.

6

Our Mountains are crown'd with imperial Oak ,
Whofe roots like our liberties, ages have nourifh'd,
But long e'er our nation fubmits to the yoke,
Not a tree fhall be left on the field where it flourifh'd
Should invafion impend,
Every grove would defcend ,
From the hill-tops they fhaded our fhores to defend ;
For ne'er will the fons &c.

7

Let our patriots deftroy Anarch's peftilent worm,
Left our Liberty's growth fhould be check'd by corrosion
Then let clouds thicken around us, we heed not ȳ ftorm.
Our realm fears no fhock but ȳ earth's own explofion.
Foes affail us in vain ,
Though their FLEETS bridge the main
For our Altars & Laws with our lives we'll maintain.
And ne'er will the fons &c.

8

Should the tempeft of WAR overfhadow our land ,
Its bolts could ne'er rend Freedom's temple afunder,
For unmov'd, at its portal would WASHINGTON ftand
And repel with his breaft, the affaults of ȳ Thunder
His fword from the fleep,
Of its fcabbard would leap,
And conduct, with its point every flafh to the deep,
For ne'er will the fons &c.

9

Let Fame to the world found America's voice,
No Intrigue can her fons from their Government fever
Her pride is her ADAMS — His laws are her choice,
And fhall flourifh till LIBERTY flumber for ever,
Then unite, heart and hand,
Like Leonidas' band,
And fwear to the GOD of the ocean and land ;
That ne'er will the fons of COLUMBIA be flaves,
While the earth bears a plant or the fea rolls its wave

NEW YORK Printed & Sold by W·HOWE Organ Builder & Importer of all kinds of Mufical Inftruments
N.º 320 Pearl Street.

W. HOWE'S EDITION (1798?) OF "ADAMS AND LIBERTY."

BALTIMORE PATRIOT *AND* *EVENING ADVERTISER.*

Tuesday Evening, Sept. 20.

BY MUNROE & FRENCH,
NO. 2, SOUTH-STREET, BALTIMORE.

THE PARTERRE.

Defence of Fort M'Henry.

The annexed song was composed under the following circumstances—A gentleman had left Baltimore, in a flag of truce for the purpose of getting released from the British fleet a friend of his, who had been captured at Marlborough. He went as far as the mouth of the Patuxent, and was not permitted to return lest the intended attack on Baltimore should be disclosed. He was therefore brought up the bay to the mouth of the Patapsco, where the flag vessel was kept under the guns of a frigate, and he was compelled to witness the bombardment of Fort M'Henry, which the Admiral had boasted that he would carry in a few hours...

O! say can you see, by the dawn's early light,
What so proudly we hail'd at the twilight's last gleaming,
Whose broad stripes and bright stars through the perilous fight,
O'er the ramparts we watch'd, were so gallantly streaming?
And the Rocket's red glare, the Bombs bursting in air,
Gave proof through the night that our Flag was still there?
O! say, does that star-spangled Banner yet wave,
O'er the Land of the free, and the home of the brave?

Tune—ANACREON IN HEAVEN.

BALTIMORE PATRIOT *AND* *EVENING ADVERTISER.*

Tuesday Evening, Sept. 20.

TO THE PUBLIC.

GENERAL ORDERS.

THE EARLIEST DATED PUBLICATION OF THE "STAR SPANGLED BANNER" TEXT.

DEFENCE
FORT M'HENRY.

The annexed song was composed under the following circumstances—A gentleman had left Baltimore, in a flag of truce for the purpose of getting released from the British fleet a friend of his who had been captured at Marlborough.—He ventured as far as the mouth of the Patapsco, and was not permitted to return lest the intended attack on Baltimore should be disclosed. He was therefore brought up the Bay to the mouth of the Patapsco, where the flag vessel was kept under the guns of a frigate, and he was compelled to witness the bombardment of Fort M'Henry, which the Admiral had boasted that he would carry in a few hours, and that the city must fall. He watched the flag at the fort through the whole day with an anxiety that can be better felt than described, until the night prevented him from seeing it. In the night he watched the Bomb Shells, and at early dawn his eye was again greeted by the proudly waving flag of his country.

*Tune—*ANACREON IN HEAVEN.

O! say can you see by the dawn's early light,
What so proudly we hailed at the twilight's last gleaming,
Whose broad stripes and bright stars through the perilous fight,
O'er the ramparts we watch'd, were so gallantly streaming?
And the Rockets' red glare, the Bombs bursting in air,
Gave proof through the night, that our Flag was still there;
O! say does that star-spangled Banner yet wave,
O'er the Land of the free, and the home of the brave?

On the shore dimly seen through the mists of the deep,
Where the foe's haughty host in dread silence reposes,
What is that which the breeze, o'er the towering steep,
As it fitfully blows, half conceals, half discloses?
Now it catches the gleam of the morning's first beam,
In full glory reflected now shines in the stream,
'Tis the star spangled banner, O! long may it wave
O'er the land of the free and the home of the brave.

And where is that band who so vauntingly swore
That the havoc of war and the battle's confusion,
A home and a country, should leave us no more?
Their blood has washed out their foul footsteps' pollution.
No refuge could save the hireling and slave,
From the terror of flight or the gloom of the grave,
And the star-spangled banner in triumph doth wave,
O'er the Land of the Free, and the Home of the Brave.

O! thus be it ever when freemen shall stand
Between their lov'd homes, and the war's desolation,
Blest with vict'ry and peace, may the Heav'n rescued land,
Praise the Power that hath made and preserv'd us a nation!
Then conquer we must, when our cause it is just,
And this be our motto—'In God is our Trust'
And the star-spangled Banner in triumph shall wave,
O'er the Land of the Free, and the Home of the Brave.

FROM THE NATIONAL INTELLIGENCER.

WASHINGTON, Sept. 16.

Copy of a letter from Capt. C. Morris to the Secretary of the Navy, dated
Portland, Sept. 3, 1814.

SIR—It is with regret that I inform you we were compelled to destroy the Adams at Hampden, on the morning of the 3d inst to prevent her falling into the hands of the enemy.

All the officers effected their escape, and I believe the crew, with the exception of very few, who were unable to travel. Their precise number cannot yet be ascertained, as we were obliged to pursue different routes, for the purpose of obtaining provisions through the woods between the Penobscot and Kennebeck.

I am now engaged collecting and forwarding the men with the utmost despatch to Portsmouth, from which place I hope soon to forward a detailed account of our proceedings. In the mean time, I request you to believe that the officers and crew of the ship reflected no immon in their power for her defense.

Very respectfully, your ob't serv't,
C. MORRIS.

The Hon. WM. JONES,
Secretary of the Navy.

CONGRESS UNITED STATES.

MONDAY, SEPT. 19.

This being the day assigned by the Proclamation of the President for the Meeting of Congress, the Members assembled at the apartments prepared for their accommodation at the usual hour. These rooms, though far from being as commodious as those heretofore occupied by the two houses, are yet much more comfortable than could have been expected from the exterior appearance of the building in which they are situated, and have been very neatly and expeditiously fitted up under the direction of the Superintendant of the city.

IN SENATE.

The Vice President not having arrived, the Hon. John Gaillard, of South Carolina, resumed the Chair as President pro tempore of the Senate.

HOUSE OF REPRESENTATIVES.

The Speaker [Hon. Langdon Cheves] took the chair and at 12 o'clock; and the roll being called, it appeared that the following members were present, viz:

INCREASE OF APPETITE.

BOSTON, Sept. 15.

When the war commenced, the enemy, promised to respect Eastport; but they afterwards took it, and then declared they meant to trouble no place to the westward of it.—They have however now taken Castine, and claim all from Passamaquoddy to Penobscot, but utter assurances that they mean to molest no other part of Maine, and these assurances will probably be about as sincere as former ones.

BRITISH THREATS.

HALIFAX, Aug. 27.

It is understood, that the grand expedition preparing at Bordeaux for America under the gallant Lord Hill, is destined for the Chesapeake direct.

VIDETTE INTELLIGENCE.

Received on Saturday evening.
WILMINGTON, Sept. 17, 1814.

Sir—I have just been informed by sailing master John Kitts, of the U. S. navy, that two heavy ships were at anchor in the Delaware, also three standing towards them.

Your humble servant,
EDWARD TWELLS, Vidette.

THE TEXT AS PRINTED IN THE BALTIMORE AMERICAN, SEPTEMBER 21, 1814.

DEFENCE OF FORT M'HENRY.

The annexed song was composed under the following circumstances—
A gentleman had left Baltimore, in a flag of truce for the purpose of getting released from the British fleet, a friend of his who had been captured
at Marlborough.—He went as far as the mouth of the Patuxent, and was
not permitted to return lest the intended attack on Baltimore should be
disclosed. He was therefore brought up the Bay to the mouth of the Patapsco, where the flag vessel was kept under the guns of a frigate, and
he was compelled to witness the bombardment of Fort M'Henry, which
the Admiral had boasted that he would carry in a few hours, and
that the city must fall. He watched the flag at the Fort through the
whole day with an anxiety that can be better felt than described, until
the night prevented him from seeing it. In the night he watched the Bomb
Shells, and at early dawn his eye was again greeted by the proudly waving
flag of his country.

Tune—ANACREON IN HEAVEN.

O! say can you see by the dawn's early light,
   What so proudly we hailed at the twilight's last gleaming,
Whose broad stripes and bright stars through the perilous fight,
   O'er the ramparts we watch'd, were so gallantly streaming?
And the Rockets' red glare, the Bomb bursting in air,
Gave proof through the night that our Flag was still there;

   O! say does that star-spangled Banner yet wave,
      O'er the Land of the free, and the home of the brave?

On the shore dimly seen through the mists of the deep,
   Where the foe's haughty host in dread silence reposes,
What is that which the breeze, o'er the towering steep,
   As it fitfully blows, half conceals, half discloses?
Now it catches the gleam of the morning's first beam,
In full glory reflected new shines in the stream,

   'Tis the star spangled banner, O! long may it wave
      O'er the land of the free and the home of the brave.

And where is that band who so vauntingly swore
   That the havoc of war and the battle's confusion,
A home and a country, shall leave us no more?
   Their blood has washed out their foul footsteps pollution.
No refuge could save the hireling and slave,
From the terror of flight or the gloom of the grave,

   And the star-spangled banner in triumph doth wave,
      O'er the Land of the Free, and the Home of the Brave.

O! thus be it ever when freemen shall stand,
   Between their lov'd home, and the war's desolation,
Blest with vict'ry and peace, may the Heav'n rescued land,
   Praise the Power that hath made and preserv'd us a nation!
Then conquer we must, when our cause it is just,
And this be our motto—" In God is our Trust;"

   And the star-spangled Banner in triumph shall wave,
      O'er the Land of the Free, and the Home of the Brave.

THE ORIGINAL BROADSIDE ("HANDBILL") OF KEY'S POEM.

O say can you see, ~~through the~~ by the dawn's early light,
What so proudly we hail'd at the twilight's last gleaming,
Whose broad stripes & bright stars through the perilous fight
O'er the ramparts we watch'd, were so gallantly streaming?
And the rocket's red glare, the bomb bursting in air,
Gave proof through the night that our flag was still there,
O say does that star spangled banner yet wave
O'er the land of the free & the home of the brave?

On the shore dimly seen through the mists of the deep,
Where the foe's haughty host in dread silence reposes,
What is that which the breeze, o'er the towering steep,
As it fitfully blows, half conceals, half discloses?
Now it catches the gleam of the morning's first beam,
In full glory reflected now shines in the stream,
'Tis the star-spangled banner — O long may it wave
O'er the land of the free & the home of the brave!

And where is that band who so vauntingly swore,
That the havoc of war & the battle's confusion
A home & a Country should leave us no more?
Their blood has wash'd out their foul footstep's pollution.
No refuge could save the hireling & slave
From the terror of flight or the gloom of the grave,
And the star-spangled banner in triumph doth wave
O'er the land of the free & the home of the brave.

O thus be it ever when freemen shall stand
Between their lov'd home & the war's desolation,
Blest with vict'ry & peace may the heav'n rescued land
Praise the power that hath made & preserv'd us a nation!
Then conquer we must, when our cause it is just,
And this be our motto — "In God is our trust,"
And the star-spangled banner in triumph shall wave
O'er the land of the free & the home of the brave.

THE ORIGINAL MANUSCRIPT OF THE FINAL TEXT OF FRANCIS SCOTT KEY'S "STAR SPANGLED BANNER."

O say, can you see by the dawn's early light
What so proudly we hail'd at the twilight's last gleaming,
Whose broad stripes and bright stars, through the clouds of the fight,
O'er the ramparts we watch'd were so gallantly streaming?
And the rocket's red glare – the bomb bursting in air
Gave proof through the night that our flag was still there.
O say, does that star-spangled banner yet wave
O'er the Land of the free & the home of the brave? –

On that shore, dimly seen through the mists of the deep,
Where the foe's haughty host in dread silence reposes,
What is that, which the breeze, o'er the towering steep
As it fitfully blows, half conceals, half discloses?
Now it catches the gleam – of the morning's first beam,
In full glory reflected, now shines in the stream,
'Tis the Star-spangled banner – O long may it wave
O'er the Land of the free & the home of the brave!

And where are the foes that so vauntingly swore
That the havoc of war & the battle's confusion
A home and a Country should leave us no more?
Their blood has wash'd out their foul footstep's pollution.
No refuge could save – the hireling & slave
From the terror of flight, or the gloom of the grave,
And the star-spangled banner in triumph doth wave
O'er the Land of the free & the home of the brave.

O! thus be it ever! when freemen shall stand
Between their loved homes & the war's desolation.
Blest with vict'ry & peace, may the heav'n-rescued land
Praise the power that hath made and preserved us, a nation.
Then conquer we must — when our cause it is just,
And this be our motto — in God is our trust —
And the star-spangled banner in triumph shall wave
O'er the land of the free & the home of the brave.

F S Key

To Gen Keim.

THE KEIM AUTOGRAPH (CA. 1842), IN POSSESSION OF THE PENNSYLVANIA HISTORICAL SOCIETY.

The Star-Spangled banner.

O! say, can ye see by the dawn's early light
What so proudly we hail'd by the twilight's last gleaming?
Whose bright stars & broad stripes, through the clouds of the fight,
O'er the ramparts we watch'd were so gallantly streaming?
And the rocket's red glare, the bombs bursting in air,
Gave proof through the night that our flag was still there.
O! say does that star-spangled banner yet wave
O'er the land of the free & the home of the brave?

On that shore, dimly seen through the mists of the deep,
Where the foe's haughty host in dread silence reposes,
What is that which the breeze, o'er the towering steep,
As it fitfully blows, half-conceals, half-discloses?
Now it catches the gleam of the morning's first beam,
In full glory reflected, now shines on the stream.
'Tis the star-spangled banner — O! long may it wave
O'er the land of the free & the home of the brave.

And where is that host that so vauntingly swore
That the havoc of war & the battle's confusion
A home & a country should leave us no more?
Their blood has wash'd out their foul footstep's pollution.
No refuge could save the hireling & slave
From the terror of flight or the gloom of the grave.
And the star-spangled banner in triumph doth wave
O'er the land of the free & the home of the brave.

O! thus be it ever when freemen shall stand
Between their lov'd homes & the war's desolation.
Blest with vict'ry & peace, may the heav'n rescued land
Praise the power that hath made & preserv'd us a nation.
Then conquer we must — when our cause it is just,
And this be our motto — In God is our trust.
And the star-spangled banner in triumph shall wave
O'er the land of the free and the home of the brave.

Washington
Oct 21 — 40.

F S Key

CIST AUTOGRAPH.

PLATE XX.

Star Spangled Banner.

36

FROM THE "NEW YORK NORMAL SONG BOOK," 1851.

Nº 12.—THE STAR-SPANGLED BANNER—CHORUS.

PLATE XXI.

Star Spangled Banner.

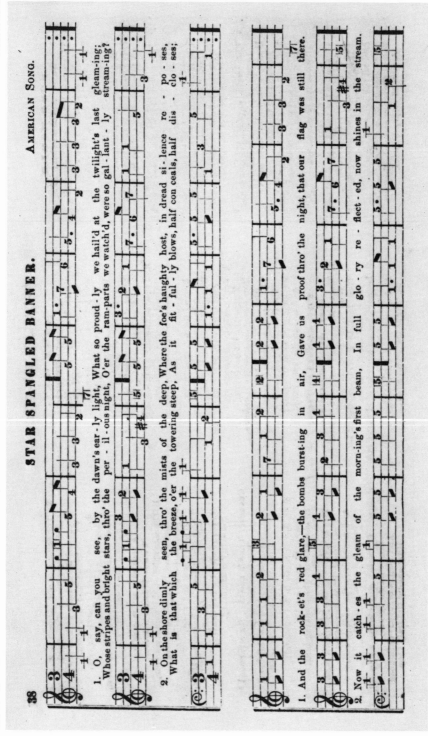

STAR SPANGLED BANNER.

AMERICAN SONG.

FROM "FILLMORE'S NEW NIGHTINGALE . . . ON A MATHEMATICALLY CONSTRUCTED PLAN OF NOTATION," CINCINNATI, 1857.

FROM "THE VOCALIST'S POCKET COMPANION," CHAMBERSBURG, 1839 ("BUCKWHEAT" OR "PATENT" NOTES).

Star Spangled Banner.

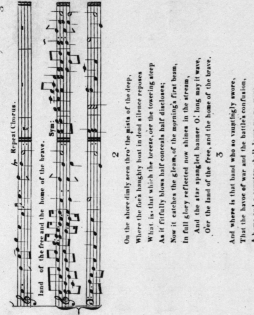

Repeat Chorus.

land of the free and the home of the brave.

Sym:

2

On the shore dimly seen thro' the mists of the deep,
Where the foe's haughty host in dread silence reposes,
What is, that which the breeze, o'er the towering steep
As it fitfully blows half conceals half discloses;
Now it catches the gleam, of the morning's first beam,
In full glory reflected now shines in the stream,
And the star spangled banner O! long may it wave,
O'er the land of the free, and the home of the brave.

3

And where is that band who so vauntingly swore,
That the havoc of war and the battle's confusion,
A home and a country shall leave us no more,
Their blood has wash'd out their foul footsteps pollution
No refuge could save, the hireling and slave,
From the terror of flight or the gloom of the grave,
And the star spangled banner in triumph doth wave
O'er the land of the free, and the home of the brave.

4

O thus be it ever when freemen shall stand,
Between their lov'd home, and the wars desolation,
Blest with vict'ry and peace, may the heav'n rescued land,
Praise the pow'r that hath made and preserv'd us a nation.
Then conquer we must, when our cause it is just,
And this be our motto— In God is our trust;
And the star spangled banner in triumph shall wave,
O'er the land of the free, and the home of the brave.

Star Spangle. 3.

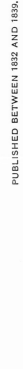

2

proud-ly we hail'd at the twilight's last gleaming,Whose broad stripes & bright stars thro' the
pe—ri—lous fight O'er the ramparts we watch'd were so gal-lant-ly streaming, And the
rocket's red glare the bombs bursting in air, Gave proof thro' the night that our
flag still was there: O! say does that star spangled ban—ner yet wave,O'er the

Star Spangle. 3.

PUBLISHED BETWEEN 1832 AND 1839.

The Star Spangled Banner

NEW YORK: PUBLISHED BY GEIB & CO Nº 23 MAIDEN LANE.

PLATE XXV.

3

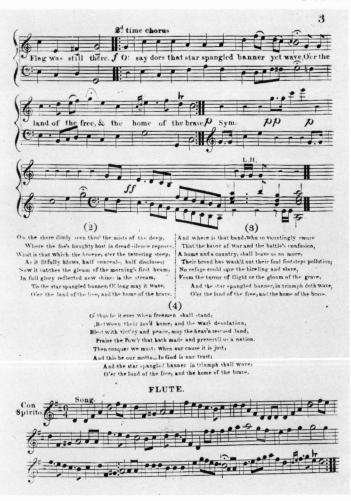

2ᵈ time chorus

Flag was still there. _f_ O! say does that star spangled banner yet wave O'er the land of the free, & the home of the brave _p_ Sym: _pp pp_ _p_

(2)

On the shore dimly seen thro' the mists of the deep,
Where the foe's haughty host in dread silence reposes,
What is that which the breeze, o'er the towering steep,
As it fitfully blows, half conceals, half discloses;
Now it catches the gleam of the morning's first beam,
In full glory reflected new shines in the stream,
Tis the star spangled banner, O! long may it wave,
O'er the land of the free, and the home of the brave.

(3)

And where is that band, who so vauntingly swore
That the havoc of war and the battle's confusion,
A home and a country, shall leave us no more,
Their brood has wash'd out their foul footsteps pollution;
No refuge could save the hireling and slave,
From the terror of flight or the gloom of the grave,
And the star spangled banner, in triumph doth wave,
O'er the land of the free, and the home of the brave.

(4)

O! thus be it ever when freemen shall stand,
Between their lov'd home, and the war's desolation,
Blest with vict'ry and peace, may the heav'n rescued land,
Praise the Pow'r that hath made and preserv'd us a nation.
Then conquer we must, when our cause it is just,
And this be our motto — In God is our trust;
And the star spangled banner in triumph shall wave,
O'er the land of the free, and the home of the brave.

FLUTE.

Con Spirito. Song.